MW00593398

The Brave In-Between

NOTES FROM THE LAST ROOM

Amy Low

NEW YORK

This is a work of creative nonfiction. While the events are true, they may not be entirely factual. They reflect the author's recollections of experiences over time. Some names and identifying details have been changed, some events have been compressed, and some conversations have been reconstructed.

Copyright © 2024 by Amy Low
Cover design by Robin Bilardello
Cover copyright © 2024 by Hachette Book Group, Inc.

Hachette Book Group supports the right to free expression and the value of copyright. The purpose of copyright is to encourage writers and artists to produce the creative works that enrich our culture.

The scanning, uploading, and distribution of this book without permission is a theft of the author's intellectual property. If you would like permission to use material from the book (other than for review purposes), please contact Permissions@hbgusa.com. Thank you for your support of the author's rights.

Hachette Books
Hachette Book Group
1290 Avenue of the Americas
New York, NY 10104
HachetteBooks.com
Twitter.com/HachetteBooks
Instagram.com/HachetteBooks

First Edition: June 2024

Published by Hachette Books, an imprint of Hachette Book Group, Inc. The Hachette Books name and logo are trademarks of the Hachette Book Group.

The Hachette Speakers Bureau provides a wide range of authors for speaking events. To find out more, visit hachettespeakersbureau.com or email HachetteSpeakers@hbgusa.com.

Books by Hachette Books may be purchased in bulk for business, educational, or promotional use. For information, please contact your local bookseller or email the Hachette Book Group Special Markets Department at Special.Markets@hbgusa.com.

The publisher is not responsible for websites (or their content) that are not owned by the publisher.

Print book interior design by Sheryl Kober

Library of Congress Cataloging-in-Publication Data

Name: Low, Amy, author.
Title: The brave in-between: notes from the last room / Amy Low.
Description: First edition. | New York: Hachette Books, 2024.
Identifiers: LCCN 2023041343 | ISBN 9780306831799 (hardcover) | ISBN 9780306831805 (paperback) | ISBN 9780306831812 (ebook)
Subjects: LCSH: Low, Amy. | Colon (Anatomy)—Cancer—Patients—Biography. | Terminally ill—Biography. | Cancer—Religious aspects—Christianity. | Christian women—Conduct of life.
Classification: LCC RC280.C6 L69 2024 | DDC 616.99/4347—dc23/eng/20240123
LC record available at https://lccn.loc.gov/2023041343

ISBNs: 978-0-306-83179-9 (hardcover); 978-0-306-83181-2 (ebook)

Printed in the United States of America

LSC-H

Printing 1, 2024

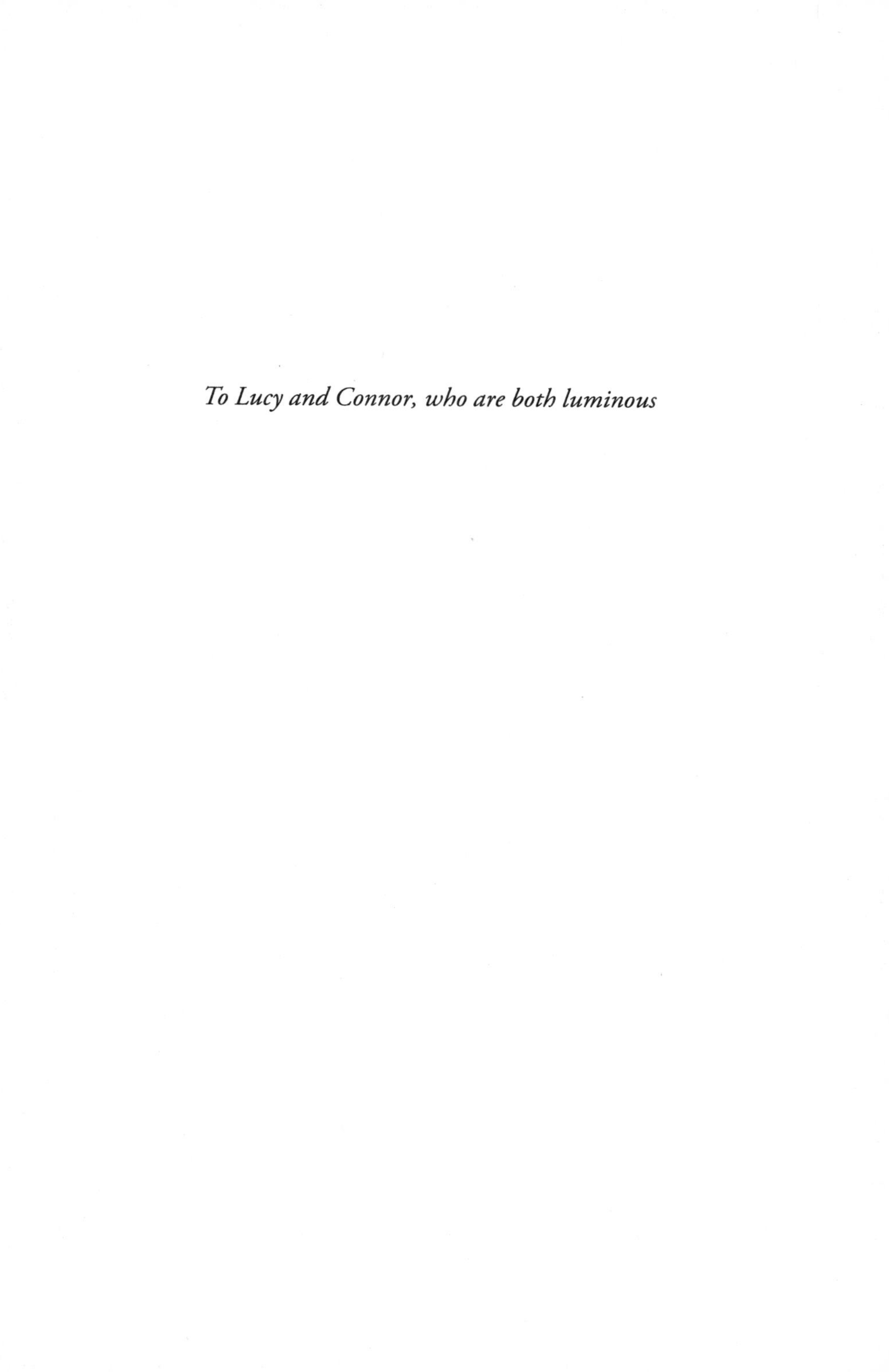

To Lucy and Connor, who are both luminous

Here is the world... beautiful and terrible things will happen. Do not be afraid.

—Frederick Buechner

CONTENTS

Sounds

The sound is not rain,
But because it's taken less
Time for the snow to melt
Than fall, from this wooden
Rocking chair small droplets
That were once snowflakes
Tumble to the unforgiving asphalt.
There is so much to say about
Things that are fleeting.
Once, I saw a small puppy
Run down my street after
Leaves drifting in the wind.
She could not name them leaves,
& probably was running after
The smell of them more than
Their wispy beauty. But ran
She did. It's like when my son
Looked into the sky during
His first snow and said mine
As a nearly imperceptible
Cold and wet particle dropped
Into his hands like somebody's
Prayer. Or it's like the boy
In Italy, & that horn of his.

Sounds

Of all the people who stood
Around listening to those men
Blow their song into the cool
Air, only he ran for the instrument
He'd hope he'd need. Who
Cares about what songs
They played? All that matters
Is from inside some apartment
Or coffee shop or car on that
Street, the sounds were like
Sheets of rain, & of course
You'd step into that cascade.

—REGINALD DWAYNE BETTS

PROLOGUE

I'M IN THE LAST ROOM OF MY LIFE.

If our lives are a series of rooms—or chapters, or seasons—this is likely my last. I like to think of this expanse of time as a room, a true place. It's furnished with paradox: warmth mixes with ice, hope arrives like a waterfall while doubt arrives with a sneer, and miracles abound, as do crushing setbacks.

Bewilderment is constant.

More than anything, this room holds a remarkable tension between the art of living fully and the discipline of waiting well.

Most of us—the fortunate ones—arrive to this room exhausted. Maybe we are eighty-nine, and our knee has been sore for a decade. Climbing stairs is awful. Joy is still present, but so is fatigue. Some quietly enter this room with a sense of acceptance, and perhaps even accomplishment. And, ideally, the room is softly lit and full of love, even if it is lonelier than previous rooms. Elderly persons often know they are here, and hopefully they are surrounded by companionship and good care.

Others of us are residing in this room feeling extraordinarily well. The room is full of life, brightly lit, raucous, maybe cluttered, and pulsing with energy. But maybe tomorrow we will choose to take on a black-diamond ski slope, clip a hidden piece of ice, and soar straight into a tree. Life ends, unexpectedly. We never knew we were in the last room.

But I do. I do know I'm in the last room. Most days I feel quite healthy. And I'm acutely aware that I'm here.

In July 2019, I was diagnosed with stage IV metastatic colon cancer. I was forty-eight, had scant symptoms and no family history. A mild fever that would come and go, coupled with some nagging fatigue, brought me to my doctor. We went chasing all kinds of theories, but the awful news arrived within days.

I had a fifteen-centimeter tumor on my liver and some worrisome activity in my lung. The biopsy revealed colon cancer was the source.

Google "stage IV metastatic colon cancer odds" and you'll discover this grim statistic: "The five-year survival rate for stage IV colon cancer is just about 14 percent."

I'm at year four, and I'm feeling well. I'm also gravely sick. Both things are true.

Living with contradiction comes naturally to me. I'm a border dweller. Or maybe it's better to say I've pitched my tent on hundreds of bridges, the places where two worlds unite and become something new. A border implies a barrier; a bridge connotes connection between two spaces. Living in-between might feel like a lonely contradiction, but for me, it's where I feel most at home.

I'm a Christian, but in recent years I've invested a good amount of time apologizing for the conservative wing of Evangelicalism in contemporary American culture—communities seemingly more motivated by fear than love. A select few fellow Christians have changed my life. Many of my friends who subscribe to different faiths, and friends who don't hold a faith tradition at all, have taught me more about the virtues I hold dear and how to live them out. One of the great gifts of my life is the diversity of voices it includes and the vantage points I've gained from a wide continuum of individuals—my kids' teenage friends who linger at my house, venture capitalists, fellow patients, a public defender who teaches me something new every time he sends me a poem that he found a way to write in his free time.

My politics are progressive, but I am more troubled by cancel culture than I am by microaggressions that sometimes bruise those who call for absolutes.

I defend religious freedoms as vehemently as I stand up for those harmed by people of faith who choose exclusion over inclusion. And I've lived my professional life rising through workplaces outside of Christianity and where fewer rules have resulted in a more expansive culture of compassion.

This means that many of my friends are sweet and civil, but they often can't stand what each other represents. I worry about what might happen if someday they are all assembled in the same spot: the gathering would be filled with individuals who are pastors, gay rights activists, conservative columnists, social justice advocates, pro-life policy experts, reproductive freedom champions, artists, accountants, right brains and left brains, and souls most comfortable at opposite edges of our ever-widening cultural expanse.

I see beauty and profound wisdom in each of them, but the real magic happens when I discover possibilities in the spaces we share. Those vantage points often reveal something new, which is breathtaking. Hope.

In the past four years, I've had to time to wonder: *Who else has set up shop in this room the way I have today? Am I part of a large club, or is this a dwelling place for a precious few? Are there some who've been in this room—the way I am—who have something to teach me? Could they offer some companionship? Do they know how to find a deeper courage in this place that I have yet to discover?*

And what about joy? Am I unusual in that this last-room residency often brings some of the best days? The most genuine laughs? The most delicious fragrances?

Or is the joy simply a coping mechanism for the unbearableness of it all?

Is there a way to tell the difference?

These pages tell an ancient story. The themes—love, loss, gain, illness, medicine, love again, loss again, and reckoning throughout—are familiar. This territory has been trekked by billions before us.

But for me, dwelling in the last room is uncharted terrain. Within these walls, I've discovered a surgeon who wears beautifully tailored suits; the attentive art of parenting through the routine of seemingly normal days, while knowing that death hovers ever too close; outdoor music in a public square; a blue lake; a collapsible chair; and a continuous craving for someone to help me make sense of it all.

And because it's important to acknowledge our mentors, the more time I've spent in this room, the more I've discovered remarkable wisdom from those who have also inhabited this sacred space the way I have. I've chosen to lean on a first-century scribe whose letters from his own last room have uncanny relevance for these unusual days of my life.

In about AD 62, Saint Paul wrote a letter to a group of his dear friends who lived in a city called Philippi. Located northwest of the Greek island of Thasos, Philippi was a Roman colony established in 27 BC. An array of advantages made it a desirable place to live, one being that it was located along the Via Egnatia, a Roman road that ran through territory that is now modern Albania, North Macedonia, Greece, and Turkey. The route eventually connected Philippi directly to Rome. Today, most historians agree that the expressway to Rome, plus mines rich in natural resources, made Philippi a wealthy enclave with the kind of privilege that resulted in everlasting monuments: a forum and a theater large enough to hold Roman games still stand today.

Paul visited Philippi around AD 50, along with his companions Silas and Timothy, and another friend named Luke. For years, they'd been visiting different cities, getting to know the people, developing deep and lasting friendships, and sharing their belief in the best news of all, which might be summed up most simply this way: *This life we're all living? There's more to it. You're part of a magnificent story, and your character matters. The story for all of us cannot happen without you and the sacred space you were created to inhabit.*

As they developed friendships in each new community, they were establishing what historians now call "the early church." These small groups containing an eclectic mix of individuals—some Jews, some without a faith tradition, others who came from worshipping Hellenistic gods—formed new circles of belief based on Christ's teaching, with forgiveness and grace at the core. Paul and his companions created communities centered on embracing this idea of "love your neighbor as yourself," how to serve the poor, how to embrace the truest form of social justice: every life matters, equally. Paul helped set it all in motion, and as his following grew, his teachings became ever more a threat to Rome.

A quick word here on Paul. He came from an elite tribe, held a high rank in Jewish circles, and was a citizen of Rome. He didn't start out as a follower of Jesus. In the years immediately following Christ's crucifixion, he was adamant about and devoted to shutting down these growing circles of friends who were convinced Christ was the Messiah. He was sure anything to do with Jesus was a threat, especially to his own standing. Over time, his conviction morphed into outright hostility; he personally supervised stonings of early Christians. He was charismatic, provocative, and militant. Early Christians feared him, and his Jewish community of fellow power brokers probably bragged about knowing him. If there were a Twitter equivalent in the first century, he would have had a lively commenting chorus, forever egging him on to double down and elevate his sharpest rebukes.

But around five years after Christ's crucifixion, Paul (who was then known as Saul) was with some friends on his way to Damascus, searching out early Christians. His goal was to round them up and bring them back to Jerusalem, where they likely would have been arrested. But while walking down this road, the risen Jesus appeared to him. Here's how the encounter is captured in the Book of Acts:

> *As he neared Damascus on his journey, suddenly a light from heaven flashed around him. He fell to the ground and heard a voice say to him, "Saul, Saul, why do you persecute me?"*
>
> *"Who are you, Lord?" Saul asked.*
>
> *"I am Jesus, whom you are persecuting," he replied. "Now get up and go into the city, and you will be told what you must do."*
>
> *The men traveling with Saul stood there speechless; they heard the sound but did not see anyone. Paul got up from the ground, but when he opened his eyes he could see nothing. So they led him by the hand into Damascus. For three days he was blind, and did not eat or drink anything.*
>
> —ACTS 9:3–9 (NEW INTERNATIONAL VERSION)

The days following were a blur of activity and confusion. The early Christians heard that their most dreaded enemy was holed up in a room, blind, and speaking of Christ as Lord. God spoke to one of them, telling him to go see Paul, place his hands on the man's eyes, and accept this most feared antagonist as a new and mighty ally.

Paul went from being an ancient influencer to a case study in disorientation. His original Jewish community viewed him as a traitor. The early Christians wondered, was he an imposter? Or an opportunist?

Paul set off, traveling to a multitude of places, and he paired his talks with something else—community. When he arrived in a bustling city or a quiet hamlet, Paul would develop lasting friendships, relationships anchored in the art of listening, dialogue, debate, coming together. He had an advantage rare in those days, and rare in ours: Paul was a leader who came from dual subcultures that were often in opposition.

He became the very essence of a bridge dweller. Paul was Jewish *and* a citizen of Rome. He was savvy. For years, he journeyed from one city to another, making valued friends and establishing these church communities. He was good at it. He knew how to translate the tenets of Christianity into the particularities of Jewish culture in a way that was also at home with the Greek philosophy at the heart of Hellenistic norms and values.

Which brings us back to Philippi. The letter he wrote to his friends in Philippi is the most Hellenistic among what we now call Paul's epistles.

As Rome continued to feel threatened by these new communities Paul was helping to establish, he was imprisoned several times, tortured, outcast. But, being the ultimate bridge dweller, Paul played his Roman citizenship card and brought his appeal straight to Caesar—he understood his Roman citizenship as an asset, a prerogative to leverage. But Nero was souring on Paul, and the warning signs were ominous. Traveling to Rome came with risk, and Paul was imprisoned once again. From this prison cell, around AD 62, he wrote a letter to his dear friends in Philippi. Paul, likely feeling exhausted but also at the top of his game, was in his last room. And he knew it.

As a Roman citizen, Paul had a few precious rights. He also had advocates and friends who cared for him—bringing food, letters, maybe some puzzles and news of the day to his cell. But most importantly, he had his pen. Paul could write, and today we are all the beneficiaries of his words. His words from his last room. Maybe he wrote by candlelight, with a scratchy blanket wrapped around him to keep warm.

Or maybe he saw things in his last room I'm still daring to glimpse, and his view illuminated every corner. Even the colors of his guards' eyes.

Some of his letters are now famous scriptures and have become part of our shared cultural language. Some of his letters have been hotly debated. Some lines from his letters make me cringe (he was a product of his time). Some parts of his letters are lyrical, lines of joy, clarity, and encouragement.

His letter to Philippi is a treasure. It was likely his last letter to a church community he helped establish, and it's clear his heart is in every sentence. He writes about squabbles and encouragements in equal measure. We meet Lydia, a prominent Philippian businesswoman and the one who seemed to have the strongest leadership qualities in the church. We meet Epaphroditus, Paul's envoy to Philippi, whom he adored. It's the kind of letter from a dear friend any of us would be amazed to receive because it's so elegantly personal.

One sentence from this letter is now the map for the most bewildering corners of my own last room:

> *Finally, brothers and sisters, whatever is true, whatever is noble, whatever is right, whatever is pure, whatever is lovely, whatever is admirable—if anything is excellent or praiseworthy—think about such things.*
>
> —PHILIPPIANS 4:8 (NIV)

These intentions—whatever is true, noble, right; whatever is pure, lovely, admirable; anything excellent or praiseworthy—are transcendent and in all kinds of ways so lofty that few would argue with their value. But here in my last room they have become something more: they are my lights.

This last room is too often dim, but these glimmers of radiance reveal what I've known forever and what I'm seeing for the first time. I'm not discovering a soft way of discerning the darkest corners that abound with confusion. Every once in a while, one of these virtues has behaved more like a spotlight, bringing clarity to chaos.

It's tempting for this progressive white lady living in modern days to set aside a first-century provocateur's words as platitudes from another era. But here in this mystifying room, it's more evident to me than ever that Paul and I share an eternal truth: our rugged humanness. Paul's virtues have created a clarity, a reckoning for a season of my life I now understand as having three acts—each one containing characters with limitless dignity, generosity, frailty, flaws, and remarkable goodness. I've come to see these characters with a renewed sense of wonder, even as I've come to terms with the inevitable incongruity of the individual desire for courage and the fears that too often guide self-interest.

The last room is one where someday we each will reside, whether we know it or not, and it's the most human experience of all. The most magical part of our individual story is that all our unique identities are linked—sometimes directly, but more often in ways that transcend our imagination.

Each of our stories has bearing. How we live our life matters, not only for our own family and community but also for all of us. Here in my last room, a companion from twenty centuries ago has illuminated the most dimly lit corners, created windows in walls, each offering a view with an invitation: There is a new story unfolding.

Come and see.

BEDROOM

I barely made it up the stairs. Just eighteen steps, with a landing in the middle. I held on to the railing and steadied myself as I placed my feet so very gently on each new step.

My house is a small cottage, so climbing up to my room used to take me about three seconds. But this time, I was hoping to make it there in less than five minutes.

I could see into my bedroom, spotless, from the steps. Bed perfectly made, clutter minimized. Don had bought a gorgeous bouquet of flowers—I think I could even smell them from step six.

He put his hand on the small of my back and encouraged me up the last twelve steps. Don straddled that tender line—he didn't let me feel helpless by doing too much, but he didn't assume I could manage much more than a slow step at a time. He was there to catch my fall, or anything worse.

We made it to the small hallway, then my room, and he helped me into bed. My abdomen was throbbing.

This was the seventh day out from a seven-hour abdominal surgery, and I had become familiar with how pain snaked through me. It would start as a twinge, then turn into a deeper spasm. Then, within minutes, a profound ache wrapped my body in still deeper spasms.

I could sit up, but just barely. I leaned back on my pillows and looked up at Don. His gentle face, his adoring eyes. They were glistening with tears. I'd always loved this about Don. Unlike many men I have known, Don could cry easily, and beautifully. He'd cried these generous tears of gratitude when our son Connor was born; he'd been dazzled by Lucy's blonde toddler curls and twirls, and he would tear up at her sweet, prekindergarten ballet recitals too.

On July 1, 2019, when I told him my news over the phone, all I could hear were his sobs. They were heavy, and it was hard for him to find his breath.

But here sitting on my bed, he was strong and gentle. He placed his hands on my legs, which I had bent to try to find a slight shift to ease the pain that was beginning, again, to snake.

"The flowers are beautiful," I said. "Thank you for those."

"Of course," he said.

I was in yoga pants and a sweater. It was Christmas Eve, and though we don't exactly have a true winter in Menlo Park, I was cold.

"Can you turn the heater on a little?" I asked. "And I think I need to get into my pajamas or something. I'm kind of hoping to sleep if I can."

Don got up and adjusted the thermostat. "Which pajamas do you want?"

"Tracy sent me a new set not too long ago. They're light pink. They should be in the top drawer in my closet."

Don returned with the pajamas.

We glanced at each other. I was in too much pain and was too exhausted to be self-conscious. Plus, the previous days in the hospital were filled with some of the most physically invasive moments of my life, so I was well past any semblance of modesty.

No matter—he already knew every inch of me. He knew just where my lower back pinched from years of picking up our kids the lazy way. He knew how at night I used to like to cradle my left foot near his, and how this small gesture would always help me fall asleep. We'd called it my foot flop.

He knew that whenever I had a cold coming on, it would set up camp in my throat. "I think the most vulnerable part of you is your throat," he often said. "Drink tea with extra honey for that sensitive throat of yours."

Don knew my scars. All of them. He knew the invisible scars best.

"I'll need help," I said, gesturing toward the pajamas. "It's hard to stand up and it's honestly hard to do everything. I'm sorry about this," and my voice cracked. Tears flowed again.

"Sorry about what?" he said softly, and he sat on the edge of my bed.

"About being so weak. About this body breaking. All of it." I looked at the ceiling to see if that might keep the tears at bay.

"You're stronger than everyone," he said.

He lifted my arms up and gently pulled my sweater over my head. And then my T-shirt. He glanced at the vertical incision that went from my diaphragm to my belly button. It was swollen, tender, red. He was careful not to let my shirt brush too closely.

I managed to sit up and face away, and he unclasped my bra, then carefully found a way to pull my light-pink pajama top over my head.

Somehow I pulled off my yoga pants while he sat on the floor ready to steer my feet into the pajamas. It was all a delicate set of careful maneuvers, guided by Don's perfect hands. His hands were the best hands I'd ever known. Long, strong fingers. A palm for me to slide mine into, like a key uniquely molded for a one-of-a-kind lock. At his best, he could stand at the front of a room and use those hands to persuade, to make a point, and all assembled would find their way into the palms of his hands as invited and captivated guests.

For many years, those hands were my home.

The snake was rising, and the spasm was on the move, becoming a throbbing ache.

"I'll need a pain pill soon, I think," I whispered.

"Of course." He reached for the pharmacy bag he'd carried up.

"But I think it's too soon," I said. "I think I had one at noon when I was discharged, and it's only two o'clock, I think."

"It's nearly three o'clock," he said. "Let's see if you can hold on one more hour."

"There's something else. I'm going to need help with this, because it might be the worst thing of all," I said, gesturing to my hospital bag. "Inside my bag you'll see a box of syringes—remember them?"

The syringes contained Lovenox, a blood thinner disguised as a door prize from the hospital to ensure I didn't develop a blood clot. I was told to inject it into my stomach twice a day. After all that I had endured, a simple injection should have been inconsequential, but the needle had a stinging kick, and I despised it.

Don knew these injections intimately. Ten years earlier, a pulmonary embolism had exploded in his lungs on a day that began with his complaining about something odd—not being able to inhale deeply for some reason—and ended in the ER with him fighting for his life. I'd barely been able to breathe at the very idea of losing him. He had recovered and come home with a box of syringes, too. He never once complained about them.

I, meanwhile, could only stare at the imposing box; each shot represented a merciless and unfair reminder that, even though I was home, I was nowhere near safe.

"Can you please do the injection?" I asked. "For some reason it hurts a tiny bit less if I look away, and you're better at this than I am."

"Of course," he said.

He got up, pulled out the box, and placed it on my nightstand. He removed one syringe and found a sterilization wipe. He softly lifted my pajama top.

"Right side or left?" he asked. He remembered that the injections needed to alternate from one side of my tender belly to the other.

"Right, I think. I forget. I guess, right."

He wiped down a little spot on my right side, pinched up a little of my abdomen, and reminded me to turn my head.

He was quick about it, knowing that getting it done and over with was the only way. I winced and cried again.

He held my hand and stared into my eyes. "I'm so very sorry," he said. "Sorry for all of this. You didn't deserve any of this," again with tears.

I stared out my window. Then, panic.

"Don. Don, I need to get up. Fast. I've got to get to the bathroom. Oh, God. Please, God, please, no," I gasped.

The next handful of minutes were a blur of me dropping onto bathroom tiles, having missed the toilet, and sobbing in the realization that abdominal surgery had resulted in a digestive system that could sleep for days but had chosen that moment to wake up.

I have never been more vulnerable as when Don cleaned me up, dressed me in new pajamas, and gently cared for me. Sprawling on my bathroom floor was a surrender, a broken body and a broken heart whose only response was to receive tenderness—with gratitude—from the most complicated person in my life.

I don't know how I ended up back in my bed. Did he carry me?

"Let's get you one more blanket." I remember him saying that. "And I think it's time for that pain pill."

I heard Connor and Lucy arrive home. Had they been out Christmas shopping?

I grabbed for Don's hand. "Don?"

"Yes?"

"Can I sleep now? Can I see the kids a little later? Is that okay? Can I sleep?"

He stroked my head, wiping my hair away from my eyes. I hadn't sat with him or spoken with him for anything more than small talk in more than five years, but our gentle gestures came naturally; they resided in our shared muscle memory of how to best care for each other. Our eyes met, seeing each other as we once miraculously were but could never be again.

"Yes, you can sleep for as long as you like. I'll start making some dinner—maybe you'll want some soup later. We'll keep it quiet downstairs."

I heard Connor settling in to play the piano, but it wasn't the right time. Don glanced up.

The pain medicine was beginning to soften the snake.

"Maybe I'll dream," I said. "I love hearing Connor play, but maybe he can play softly."

Don, my ex-husband, let go of my hand. He stood up and left my bedroom, where he was now simply a guest.

Whatever Is True

THIS STORY BEGINS WITH AN AWFUL ENDING.

One of the many things I never considered when I was married was how to share hard news with our kids as a solo agent. Within a partnership, those kinds of conversations get rehearsed over bathroom sinks, while one parent is flossing and the other is drying off. Or late at night, in bed, when the most sacred conversations happen. Full of trust, a shared history, and a common vision.

Single parents must navigate those hard talks differently. Friends can weigh in, of course; so can family. But nothing prepares you to stare down those uniquely intimate mysteries that move through conversations between a single parent and her kids that are magically—and oftentimes, unbearably—private. What's unspoken can guide a dinner conversation. What's said plainly can be lost by the time baseball practice is over.

A late-night whisper during a bedtime tuck-in can last a lifetime.

That intimate family language no longer lives between two adults doing their best to raise children entrusted to them and no one else.

How does anyone, unaccompanied, share the most devasting news of all?

In 2010, I was married to the love of my life. We had a seven-year-old son and a five-year-old daughter; Don's daughter from his first marriage was seventeen and making plans for college. My career was challenging and deeply satisfying. Our life was joyful, stressful, delightful, chaotic—a mix of paradoxes that I adored calling home.

We lived on Magnolia, in Seattle, where the glistening views of Elliott Bay are part of a simple commute to downtown.

Friends and dinner parties and spontaneous laughter were part of our rhythm.

But underneath, a terrible darkness had taken hold. The fallout of the Great Recession meant that Don's once-successful advertising agency had shuttered its doors after several unsuccessful attempts to find a buyer. He pivoted quickly to consulting, signing on a range of clients to keep his days full. But his ego was badly bruised. The plan for his life, a vision of stature and economic stability, began to crumble.

The reality of his life—a wife who loved him fully, healthy children, and a vibrant circle of friends—was beautifully intact. Our family life was a mix of satisfying and exhausting.

Mother's Day 2012. Don got up early to make me breakfast in bed, with the kids, ages nine and seven, doing their best to contribute to pancake decorating and juice pouring. The joy train arrived in our bedroom, a tray of food and coffee and small gifts. I reached for Don's card first, excited to see what wonderful expression of his ardor and humor he'd come up with this time. But it simply said, "In it all, you're a great mom." My breath caught in my chest. Something more than a bruised ego was off. He knew how much his words meant to me, and he chose to withhold them.

We'd built the first year of our romance with words by exchanging long letters while I was living in New York City and he was in Seattle.

Don and I had attended the same small college, but he was eleven years older than me, and we'd first met at an alumni event a couple of years after I graduated. He lived in Seattle and was married with a young daughter. A few years later, we reconnected and he shared that his marriage was ending. As he was moving through a tough season, we developed an email friendship, which later blossomed into a long-distance romance once his divorce proceedings were underway. For our first-year anniversary, I'd printed out all the letters and bound them into a book for us, a keepsake we treasured.

As my New York project concluded, I was elated to move to Seattle to see whether our romance would be as captivating living in the same city as it was with three thousand miles between us. I found a small apartment on Lake Union; it was important for me to have my own place at first. I wanted to create a relationship with my future stepdaughter based on what I thought were the best decisions I could make, one of which was to not immediately move into her home with her dad, especially because he and I were still dating and discovering if our relationship was strong enough for the long term.

Once I moved to Seattle, our words became even more magical. Our conversations waltzed. The flourishes and twists and nuances that were once part of our long-distance phone calls became treasured gems, some that found their way into our secret marriage language, carefully wrapped packages we created uniquely for us.

I think I have a crush on you, I'd say while washing the dishes after a long day, looking at him in a way that would restore sweetness for the evening. *Ravish* was our word for romance. We'd meet for a spontaneous lunch on Lake Union, and I'd settle into our booth with *Have I ever told you you look like a movie star today?* He called me *Peach* because our first date had spilled into the next day and a drive to Napa, where I told him the best taste in the world was a summer peach so sweet I couldn't help but twirl with every messy bite. When my brow was furrowed, Don had a way of running his fingers across my temple and saying, *You seem to be missing your sorts. Let's see if we can find them for you.*

Our refrains were touchpoints, the important daily deposits that kept our love account growing. A way of returning us to the frothy days of our origin story. Or at least that was what I thought.

When I read that terse Mother's Day card, I realized Don had made a choice to abandon our words, our intimacy. Suddenly, I knew this wasn't a grim professional season or some kind of midlife sorrow. This was something far worse.

By Christmas of that year, the shadows enveloping our beautiful home became as heavy as the drudge of a Seattle winter: a pervasive gray and biting mist, occasional winds that could knock anyone off their feet.

Desperate to reset everything—by which I meant Don's outlook and its impact on our family—I cashed in all of my air miles from work trips to India and China and bought him a first-class ticket to the Italian Cycling Center, solo. A time to recharge, I thought. A time for him to remember how lovely I was, how I was still capable of tending the garden of us with sacrifice and loving care.

Sitting next to our sparkly Christmas tree, he read the ticket and my card and cried a little. But they weren't tears of gratitude. Just sadness. My mom glanced at me with a heartbroken look, and I decided to fetch more coffee for everyone.

Later that afternoon, Don and I went to see *Les Misérables*, which had just opened. We both adored the story. We'd even given our daughter Lucy the middle name Marais (which I found out later actually means "swamp"; someday she'll forgive me).

Sitting there in the dark theater, Don's hand in mine, I got lost in memories of our trips to France. How in 2004 we'd watched the final stage of the Tour de France sitting with thousands of others on the Champs-Élysées. But as Anne Hathaway began her soul-crushing solo "I Dreamed a Dream," Don bolted up and went to stand in the back of the theater. I twisted around in my seat, watched him crouched with his hands on his face, and knew in my gut that I had lost him.

A week later, the kids were still out of school, but Don and I were back to work. He kissed me on the cheek and left me in our bathroom staring at the counter, where he'd inadvertently left his phone.

It didn't take long. Only a few taps and I found a Yahoo! email account I didn't recognize. In it were hundreds of emails and photos, more than any spouse should ever see. Beautiful and intimate exchanges—containing phrases that had been part of our secret marriage language.

The most recent message was from only hours earlier, promises of an overdue rendezvous in Portland on Friday, with Christmas gifts.

The house phone rang, and Don's office number appeared on the caller ID. I picked up, sank to the floor, and simply began reading the emails to him.

He told me, panic in his voice, he was coming right home. I kept reading the emails.

He hung up, and I knew I didn't have much time until he arrived. I frantically rallied my nanny and asked her to please take the kids away—anywhere, the park, anywhere. I didn't want them to see or hear us.

But I, too, wanted to flee. To flee all the deception and this implosion, in real time, of my life.

I tried to pack a bag, but I was too late—his car was pulling in. I burrowed into our closet, took off my wedding ring, and wailed. He found me there and began an incoherent conversation about how—now—it was finally going to end. How he'd let a harmless flirtation run amok. How he was relieved, and how he would now be released from this hell he'd been living in.

"Did you tell her you loved her?"

"Yes," he said. "But it's over now."

"But just ten hours ago you emailed her about your upcoming rendezvous."

"Yes," he said. "But I was planning on ending it then. I want our family to continue. I want you. I love you. I was in an awful and dark place, but now we can begin again."

"Really," I said. "Okay. Well, why don't you call her and end it right now? Go ahead and put it on speaker so I can hear." I threw the phone at him, and incredibly, he dialed her number, put it on speaker.

"Hi, babe," she cooed.

"Hi. Uh, so, listen. Amy knows everything now. So, we have to end this, and end it now."

"Wait, what?" she cried. "What do you mean?"

"I mean—I love my wife. And we have to end this." And with that, he hung up.

I curled up in a ball in our bedroom, barely able to breathe, and wondered, *What on earth comes next?*

The days and weeks after the implosion were a mix of horror and routine. Dinners still needed to be made, second-grade spelling tests still needed signatures, work meetings persisted. But sprints to the bathroom to cry—whether at home or during a work lunch—were part of the new normal.

So was the urgent quest for truth. A quest so urgent, it superseded all else. I needed to understand what had happened to me—to the life I thought I was living and the family I thought I was making. For months, I wondered if I would ever reconcile these two paradoxical truths—did the discovery of Don's separate life invalidate the life I had made with him?

In the virtues that Paul lists from his last room, he begins with truth. This is by design. Paul understood that truth is the chassis for all the other virtues. None can flourish, can be lived, without clarity about the facts of our lives.

Within our lived days, our facts are our moments. They are mundane—a trip to the vet or a bill paid. And they are marvelous—an anniversary or the way a professor in a college history class provides a new insight about the Enlightenment. In between the mundane and the marvelous, the moments build to become our story; hour upon hour, our story becomes our treasured, most intimate, personal narrative.

The agony of betrayal is that your story—or what you thought was your story—is brazenly stripped away by the one you trusted the most to care for it. The story I'd built with Don—where he was when he said he was golfing, where he led me to believe we were as a couple, where we were headed as a family—evaporated.

My deepest story, the most intimate part of any soul, shattered. Worse, it disappeared.

If our memories form a map that points us to decisions for today and for the days to come, my map no longer held familiar markers. I was lost. Frantically, fearfully lost.

If our memories become lies, are they still memories? If your story is no longer real, is your place within it still valid?

I needed to put some semblance of my life map back together, no matter what it revealed, and so I went searching for the facts, which I thought would point me toward the truth. The golfing trip? It was a hotel room in Seattle. The work trip? It was a weekend in Palm Springs. The trips to the grocery store that for some reason took two hours? At least an hour was spent on the phone in the parking lot.

The pain that followed each revelation was always new, always searing, each fresh revelation of a lie I'd swallowed kneecapping me once more. I needed to recover the truth so that I could find a way to stand again. Don understood this, so he handed over the passwords to his phone and computer and said I could ask him anything. The back-and-forth was brutal; we'd often sit inside our walk-in closet so Connor and Lucy couldn't hear.

Don's relationship outside our marriage had lasted a staggering three years. A thousand days of our married life were a lie.

We tried mightily to recover our marriage. We were desperate to not make this fallout our forever, but desperation turned to exhaustion, and ultimately defeat.

In those final days of agony within the marriage, I would go on walks and daydream about my future. I wondered: *Would I ever wake up without feeling immediate dread?*

Slowly, an image formed of my fictional future self, one who laughed easily again. She enchanted me, a mom who delighted in her kids' good progress, a work colleague known more for creativity than wounded distraction, a friend who'd arrive for lunch ready to listen to others' stories rather than needing to sort out her own. A sister who rooted for her brother's and sister's marriages even while missing her own.

The only way to become this woman was to create a new chapter, one with truth at its core. My days with Don had been taken hostage by my frantic quest for the plot details of the previous three years, and no matter how many answers I received, they never satisfied my need to know more.

I was stuck wondering if my own shortcomings had played a role in Don's infidelity. I probed, I inquired, I blamed myself at times. Could I have been more sensitive? Or was it simply that I no longer held his affection?

Was there a truth to be discovered about myself that I needed to find?

This searching, this second-guessing, this doubt. All of it resulted in a paralysis and, worse, a coarsening of my heart. Something as simple as an exchange with a barista encouraging me to try a new summer drink had me doubting anything she was offering was sincere. I felt cynical, trapped on a journey to bitterness.

The quest for details gradually became less important than the yearning to shed my pervasive doubt. A desire to believe again and to revel in the joy of being my true self.

I came to learn the ultimate gift of truth: peace of mind. Truth enables all the other virtues to flourish. Without it, any map of our lives becomes chaotic and unreliable.

Truth is a virtue we all hold, but its absence is the only way to measure its worth.

Paul loves lists. In his correspondence to individuals and communities alike, his paragraphs unspool encouragements, admonishments, pragmatics, and generous wisdom. But he often saves his best stuff for the lists. And like any good list maker, his first entry is the vital one.

To his beloveds in Philippi, his crescendoing list begins with an encouragement to hold fast to anything that is true. I imagine, as a last-room dweller, Paul spent his days moving through his memories, recalling conversations, subtleties, mountaintop moments from his travels. His memories were his core, a compass that guided his days and his words.

What's more, Paul likely understood that his memories formed the meaning of his message, fashioned the grander story he had been called to share. Without truthful memories, Paul couldn't have earned the trust of the early churches he helped establish or shared ideas about how to live fully into the years to come.

Truth, then, creates authenticity out of memories, a coherency that enables us to understand how our past moments are linked. These links form the chapters in our story. If truth is a constant, a coherent plot emerges that reveals a deeper meaning to the story—a hope strong enough to fuel ever more chapters in our lifetime narrative.

Truth, of course, also fuels our future. We can't begin to make decisions for tomorrow without trusting the authenticity of today. In a letter Paul wrote to a young church community in Ephesus, he says, "God wants us to grow up, to speak the truth and tell it in love" (Ephesians 4:15 NIV). It's tempting to read this sentence as a simplistic encouragement, but there's more here to discover. Paul is beckoning his friends to a new place, a place for grown-ups. He's suggesting that truth telling creates durable bonds, a dependability that results in a lasting sense of satisfaction. When truth is central, relationships mature. Inevitably, these kinds of relationships will require more work and far more trust to maintain. Some conversations will be inconvenient. Others, deeply uncomfortable. And yet, within a realm of truth, endurance takes hold, one that creates an inner confidence generated by a magnificent magical paradox: as we become more attached to our beloveds, we experience ever more personal liberation.

Don and I spent nine valiant months devoted to the work of saving our marriage. In the wreckage of those many weeks, we experienced glimmers of sweetness, small tastes that would intoxicate us with the possibility that maybe our wounds would heal. But for each sweet taste, a crash of unrelenting pain would overwhelm me, slowly deadening whatever tastebuds were left in our marriage.

By July, my longing for truth had created enough courage for me to imagine my life with new memories, truthful memories. I felt a stirring to stand, to breathe, and later, a flicker of something new. A fragile knowing of an invitation to step forward, but just barely. An invitation less about an exit and more about an entrance.

Part of that entrance came in the form of a job opportunity with Emerson Collective, Laurene Powell Jobs's new venture. The role was based in Palo Alto; Don and I are both originally from California, and we had talked about how the survival of our life together might one day hinge on finding a new home, one with more of the vitamin D abundant in our childhoods.

When Palo Alto called, I understood it as a lifeline.

I wanted a new home. I wanted to wake up in a new bedroom and for the kids to have a happier mom. More than anything, I wanted a truthful life.

Don agreed that the Palo Alto opportunity was a golden one and encouraged me to take it. He assured me that he would follow me there after our Seattle house sold, either to continue our rugged work to save our marriage or to live nearby as a co-parent.

I moved quickly to find a rental house near my new office in a solid public school district so the kids could start the new academic year there.

I needed a new beginning. Don did, too. Only of a different kind.

The official decision to divorce came while Don was still in Seattle, so it fell to me to tell Connor and Lucy this awful news.

For days, I faced an impossible dilemma: tell the truth about their dad's betrayal and add to their wound, or leapfrog over it and participate in a larger set of falsehoods.

I searched for a middle path. A path that would hold the most expansive space for truth, but not destroy. In my searching I discovered that sometimes speaking truth includes not saying everything so that beloveds have the time and space to grow into wisdom. Dosing, then, is as crucial in our discourse as it is for a medical prescription.

I designed a dosage to communicate a truthful frame, one that would coexist with my decision to avoid any mention of Don's infidelity. I alone would carry the detailed story through their growing-up years in order for them to have a full and unencumbered relationship with their dad. I would carry this by myself to keep Don fully alive to his children, who adored him. That part was true. On a Friday in October 2013, I welcomed Connor and Lucy home from school and asked them to settle in with me in our living room. I had been crying. They had grown accustomed to my red, puffy face, so I led with that.

"You know I've been sad for so much of this year," I began. "And I know my sadness makes some of our days hard. I want you to know that starting today we're beginning a new chapter where hopefully my days won't be quite as sad. But it's going to be a long chapter, and it's one all three of us are going to write together."

Their perfect eight- and ten-year-old faces looked at me. Blue eyes locked with mine. I closed my eyes. And then I told them the worst thing I thought they would ever hear.

"For reasons we'll never understand, your dad's love for me changed. He decided he loves me more like Friend Love rather than Married Love. And, unfortunately, that means we can't be married anymore.

"This is awful, and I'm incredibly sad. I miss him all the time. But remember the love I told you about that moms and dads have for kids? That hasn't changed at all. And Dad is still your amazing and incredible dad. And always will be."

When I was finally able to look my cherubs in the eyes, I saw two faces washed with tears. Their young hearts had cracked open, and their world changed in an instant. Sorrow moved in, but I drew them close and tried to beat back the fear as heroically as I could.

Over the next few years, we carried our hearts forward, stumbling often. We developed new instincts, learned to catch each other, and moved into a season centered on recovering and rebuilding.

Throughout, we learned truth is a form of stewardship. A steady moving toward and communicating of what is real, with as much care and courage as we can provide.

Whatever Is Noble

Summer 2019.

He didn't bother to knock on my hospital-room door.

He was young for a doctor—maybe mid-thirties—and it was well past eleven o'clock at night. My elderly roommate had finally drifted off to sleep. She was maybe in her eighties and had fallen at her nursing home. Her medical team suspected dementia. I knew this because they entered frequently and asked the same group of questions:

"Do you know what month it is?"

"Summer," she'd say, which matched our reality.

"Do you know why you're in the hospital?"

"I'm not sure. I thought that was your job." Again, correct.

"Do you know who the president is?"

"Yes, but I don't want to say his name." Also an answer many would have given in 2019.

But the doctor who entered our room that night didn't knock. He was there for me. He walked right over to my bedside in the dark. I could only make out the shadows of his face, his white coat the only part of the room partially lit.

"I wanted you to know I've reviewed your CT scans," he said after what I think was an introduction, but I didn't catch his name. "You should know this is most likely quite serious. You should prepare. The biopsy news will possibly be grim. I thought you would want to know. You'll probably hear confirmation in the next day or two. That's all I have."

And he was gone.

I was alone with my roommate, whose name I didn't know.

The fall of 2013 ushered in uneven days as Connor, Lucy, and I slowly established a rhythm in our new home in Menlo Park. They were just starting fifth and third grades, academic seasons that gallop more than trot: Connor was devouring novels instead of slowly conquering one at a time, while Lucy maneuvered through multiple math milestones and adopted grammar rules into her new writing skills.

But just as we were starting to trust the ground under our feet, the crush of the divorce was followed—weeks later—by a new and devastating twist. Don sent me an email on a Tuesday afternoon. I had just left a meeting and resettled at my desk when I saw his name in my Gmail folder. He was letting me know that he'd decided to live in Costa Mesa.

Costa Mesa, which is 356 miles south of where we were in Menlo Park.

He explained his reasoning: he would be "a short flight away" and would "always be available" for the kids. Don was still consulting, so he was *choosing* to live hundreds of miles from his children.

My job was growing ever more complex—how would I juggle two kids on my own without a co-parent close by? I stared out the office window, thinking about the basic math problem: the cost of living in Menlo Park was exorbitant and I didn't know how I could add childcare onto my expenses. But how else would I be able to fulfill evening work obligations or weekday travel? I had chosen to live in Menlo Park because the short commute to my office enabled me to spend as much time with Connor and Lucy as possible, and because Don and I had agreed he would co-parent with me if the marriage failed.

So, by the time Don shared this news, the kids were already settled in their new school and connected to new activities. Little League and youth band for Connor, dance classes for Lucy. How could I upend the kids' lives again so abruptly, and add upward of an hour to my commute, to move to where I could afford after-school childcare when the very thing Connor and Lucy needed most was at least one parent present in the rhythm of their lives?

I drove home that night alternating between the heartbreak I felt for the kids and the panic gripping my heart around how I would make the logistics of our life come together. I was just making a few new friends in this community, but I was ashamed to admit that I had an ex-husband who would willingly choose not to live near his kids. Instead of reaching out for help, I isolated, living mostly hour to hour between work obligations and single parenting.

In the months that followed, a fragile framework for shared parenting emerged. I aimed to make sure Don had at least eight to ten days a month with the kids, which initially meant he would fly up on various weekends and the kids would stay in nearby hotels with him. At first, the novelty of it all took away some of the sting. *Our hotel has a robot that delivers room service! Our last hotel had the best pancakes at breakfast!* But I knew the sparkle of random nights in a hotel would wear off quickly, and eventually Don found a local friend with a spare bedroom where he could set up a base camp for visits.

As my travel schedule increased, I knew where this new logistical layer would lead us. I had three options: find a nanny (expensive and complicated because the kids would naturally want to be with Don when I was away), tell the kids they'd need to stay in hotels or at Don's friend's apartment (a thirty-minute-plus drive to school and they had to sleep on air mattresses), or tell Don he could stay in my house (by far the least disruptive option for the kids). Though I begged my smartest friends for an option I was missing, no one offered an alternative, and my choice became clear. I chose Connor and Lucy. Don would stay in my house when I traveled. And, of course, Don would sleep on the couch rather than in my bed.

It was never not terrible for me to call home from a trip. If I was talking to Connor, I could hear Don making dinner in the background and Lucy asking how to spell a word for her homework. I could hear my former life being fully lived in my kitchen without me. I would hang up, crawl into my hotel-room bed, confident I was making the right decision and exhausted by everything that made it right.

In the exhaustion, I found resignation. And, eventually, some degree of numbness. Peace was elusive for a long time.

However, despite his haunting our house with his presence, I rarely saw Don himself. If I was scheduled to land at four o'clock, he was likely on a flight that left an hour before I arrived. We could go months without ever crossing paths. Gradually, I felt more like a widow than a divorcée.

He was more memory than man.

As recovery slowly graduated to rebuilding, Menlo Park began to feel more like home, and life tilted more toward investing rather than surviving. Connor and Lucy developed new friend groups, found ways to embrace Silicon Valley upgrades from the home we still missed in Seattle, and I began playing tennis again with a local club.

My work with Emerson Collective matured, too. Initially, my role was focused on leading the organization's communications work, but as we grew in number, my interests evolved to include strategizing how to incubate grants for new nonprofit journalism models and—my passion—developing a fellowship portfolio for the organization. I was fortunate to work for Laurene, who encouraged all of us to have a bias toward yes and an abiding affinity for what we called "what if" questions. I asked a lot of them.

As anyone who has experienced grief or trauma knows, recovery and rebuilding are maddeningly nonlinear. For every solid week, a string of lousy days would follow.

As we learned to live with our wounds, we also experienced new ways to soar. Lucy tried out for the school play when she was eleven and ended up with the lead role. She promptly astonished me by memorizing all 270 lines to play Anne Frank. Meanwhile, Connor seemed to learn a new instrument every week, and by the time he was a freshman, he was leading the youth group band. And I felt like my career was making a lasting difference.

I began dating, which, more often than not, resulted in a range of lovely friendships with single dads, a new community of parents I was eager to know. Romances—some brief, others with a longer run—were sprinkled throughout. My heart remained open.

Then in the spring of 2019, I was attending the TED conference with a few colleagues from Emerson Collective. I'd arrived in Vancouver from a work trip in Oxford, England, so I was jet-lagged waiting for my luggage in baggage claim. I glanced at the television monitor to see live coverage of the Notre Dame Cathedral engulfed in flames and quietly wondered: *Is this a sign of some sort?* When a treasured icon is on fire, it's hard not to ponder what might happen next.

My fatigue lingered throughout the conference, which was annoying. I had a hard time tracking the speakers and an even harder time making small talk with friends while working to meet new people. I went to the gym one afternoon, and after just two miles walking uphill on the treadmill, I decided to go back to my room in the hopes of sneaking in a nap before the evening activities.

One morning I woke up drenched in sweat.

But after a hot shower and a hot cup of coffee, I felt fine, or close enough. I dismissed it all as perimenopause symptoms.

The last night of the conference I was meant to have dinner with Emerson colleagues and some invited guests, but as I sat through the final speaker session, a visceral wave of fatigue washed over me. I became preoccupied struggling to imagine how I would make the fifteen-minute walk back to my hotel room. I texted a colleague and said I'd have to miss dinner, dragged myself to my room, and crawled into bed.

The next morning, I woke up drenched again. But I managed to pack up, fly home, and sleep it off over the weekend.

In the following weeks, these physical quirks came and went. A few perfectly normal days were followed by a day or two of low-grade fever and terrible exhaustion. Then those days would pass, and a new quirk would emerge. My gut seemed off at times, and then the fevers would return.

The last weekend in May, I played in a tennis match against my club's local rivals, Woodside. Woodside matches were always brutal—they took no prisoners, we had to play on high school courts without benches or shade, and their captain would circle the courts like a hungry tiger looking for prey—think *Real Housewives* with sneaky serves.

I played singles that day and assumed my opponent would bring a typical Woodside spicy edge. But instead, she was polite and even made a passing reference to how her teammates were a bit much. We settled into the first set, but I struggled to chase after easy balls. At a changeover, she asked if I was feeling all right, and I said I was fine.

"Are you sure? You look a little flushed. I have some vitamin water if you need it."

"Oh, thanks. No, I'm fine. Just tired. I think I'm fighting some kind of bug."

"Yeah, I get that," she said. "My husband picked up a lousy bug from a recent trip to Mexico and he's been fighting it for weeks."

I walked to the other side of the court with a new thought. Two months before I'd spent a few days in Honduras for work, and maybe I'd been battling some kind of parasite? It made sense. A low-grade fever, an out-of-whack gut, fatigue. The thought gave me more pep for the second set, and I was delighted to retake the lead.

But at 5–3, the exhaustion hit me again, and the sun was scorching. I got ready to serve for the set, glanced at my teammates, and realized the very idea of staying out there for a third set was completely out of reach. I muttered as much to a teammate, and she was gracious about it. I made it through the next few games, losing gracefully, and moved as fast as my tired legs could take me to my car.

I made an appointment to see Dr. Marx, my primary care physician, the next day.

"Okay, so mild fevers and a funky gut?" she asked.

"Yes, and the fatigue. It's terrible. But then there are days I feel just fine."

"Well, you might be on to something with your parasite idea. Let's order labs to rule out other things. That fever of yours isn't a typical sign of cancer and thank goodness for that."

Had she been trying to dismiss any wild thoughts I might have been having? I wasn't having wild thoughts—I was just trying to play tennis and stay awake past eight o'clock.

Dr. Marx's lab orders revealed that my liver seemed to be struggling, so she put in an order to meet with an infectious-disease doctor. "This could be consistent with your thought about a parasite," Dr. Marx messaged me. "You may have an infection, which would also explain your odd bowel symptoms. You'll be in good hands with my referral."

I met with Dr. Jones a few days later. "You were in Honduras?" he asked. "Where, exactly?"

"I was in San Pedro Sula," I said.

"Oh, I'm not familiar with that area." He looked into my ears. "Is it rural, urban?"

"It's mostly urban—very poor. But we stayed in modern hotels, and I remember being careful with the water."

"Mm-hmm," he said, then asked to look in my throat. "What brought you there?"

"I work for an organization that has a focus on immigration reform; we were looking at what's causing so many families to flee to the United States."

"Yeah, that's such a tough problem," he said.

"Right. Okay, well, what do you think?"

"Well, that liver count is odd, so I'm going to order an ultrasound to see if there's anything suspicious there. You might have an abscess, and if so, we should find out right away."

"Okay. What if there is an abscess?" I asked.

"We'd have to drain it—not hard, but it's time sensitive. But let's not go there until we know more. In the meantime, I'm going to prescribe an antibiotic, which should help with your fever and address whatever it is that's going on."

"Got it. Okay. Nice to meet you!" I hopped off the exam table and made the appointment for the sonogram down the hall.

A few weeks prior, I'd had a lovely first date with a handsome surgeon. Sebastien and I had immediately realized that our worlds overlapped. After more than twenty years in the operating room as a senior surgeon at a prominent local hospital, he had pivoted to a corporate role with a pharmaceutical company to drive its global health-equity initiatives. He knew Emerson Collective's work, especially around cancer research and other health priorities. Our shared interests in harnessing resources and capital for good were evident within the first half hour; our shared intrigue with each other was evident within the first five minutes.

A series of equally lovely dates had followed. We went on long walks in Half Moon Bay, took in art at San Francisco's MOMA, enjoyed drinks and bites in cozy restaurant booths, and discovered a conversation and physical connection that flowed effortlessly.

We were both traveling quite a bit for work but tried to talk frequently. One day on the phone, as I was getting in my steps with my trusty water bottle in hand, I mentioned the Honduran-born infection idea to him, and we ended up chatting about the history of typhoid and ancient infections that continue to pop up, even centuries later—as one does in any new romance. He then asked, "Has your doctor ordered a stool sample?"

I stopped dead in my tracks, choking on my water. I managed a spluttering, "Umm. Yeah, not sure! I bet we'll cross that bridge if we get to it! I'm actually feeling fine today, so I bet whatever this is will just run its course!" I scrambled off the call, hoping a shred of alluring mystery was still intact.

Oh, the things I used to care about.

Two days later, I was standing in front of the small airport in Aspen when my phone rang and what's now the most familiar number popped up on the screen, the Palo Alto Medical Foundation. I picked up and asked for a minute while I climbed into the backseat of an SUV with a work colleague.

"Ms. Low? I'm calling with the results from your sonogram. You appear to have a fifteen-centimeter mass on your liver. There's a possibility this is a very large abscess and it will need to be drained, soon."

"I'm sorry, did you say fifteen centimeters? On my liver? That sounds kind of big. How big is that?" I asked in a way that I hoped sounded more breezy than panicked.

My colleague glanced my way and I realized I was having a completely normal-sounding chat about something clearly abnormal.

"Yes, well, it's sizable," Dr. Jones said. "We don't know the nature of it, but you'll need to have this addressed."

The nature of it?? "Ah, okay. Well, I'm in Aspen. Can I have this looked at in a few days?" Is fifteen centimeters more like a large grapefruit or maybe a kid-sized bowling ball?

"Uh. Probably. I would maybe come home a little earlier if you can."

"Got it. Okay. Thanks!"

Incredibly, I hung up and began chatting about the conference we were about to attend, categorizing whatever was happening to me as more inconvenient than scary.

But by the time I got to my hotel, I thought I ought to text Sebastien the technical readout of the sonogram the doctor had summarized on the phone.

> Hi. Random question! Can you look at this medical narrative? This looks suspicious and now my fever is back. Any idea what might be going on?

Sebastien immediately called instead of texting me back. "What do you mean your fever is back?"

"Well, I'm out of the antibiotic my doctor prescribed. Maybe it's back because of that?"

"Where are you exactly?"

"I'm in Aspen."

"No, I mean what street? What's your address?"

I found a notepad with the hotel address on it and within minutes he'd instructed me to get to the pharmacy down the street to refill my prescription.

"If it is an abscess, you need to stay on the antibiotic. Also, you should come home."

"Sebastien? Do you think this is serious?"

"I have no idea. Let's pray it's not anything more than an infection. But either way, I wouldn't wait too much longer."

Not anything more than an infection. A close cousin to *the nature of it.* As I signed the forms to pick up the prescription, I noticed my hands were shaking. I walked outside and called Don, knowing the next few days were likely not going to go as we'd planned.

"Hi. Listen, do you have a second?"

"Yes, what's up?" he responded.

"Well, you know how I've been having a number of tests, how I've been a little out of sorts the last few weeks?" I then caught myself, realizing that I hadn't shared so much as a hangnail with him in over six years. "What I mean is," I continued, "I've just not been feeling myself. Anyhow, a doctor just called saying I have a large mass on my liver, and I may need to come home early and have this looked at. I may even have to spend a night in the hospital."

"Oh gosh, okay," he said. "Can you get a flight home—when, like tomorrow?"

"I don't know just yet," I said. "I guess. I mean, I just got here."

"Well, the most important thing is your health. I can be with the kids as long as you need. But I do need to fly home Thursday for an important meeting—that said, if you need me to come back, of course I will."

And, suddenly, while he prevaricated, I heard it—a voice. The deeply discerning inner voice we all carry. She was telling me in what felt like a clear whisper that made the aspen leaves shimmer around me, *This is real, and you are approaching a new door. You are nearly there.*

"Don." My voice cracked. "I think this is incredibly serious. I think we have to be prepared to change a plan or two. I just don't know."

He must have heard the fear in my voice and began to reassure me, relaying the familiar platitudes of not getting ahead of the story.

But I was still listening to my intuition and she was drowning him out.

I hung up, walked over to the aspen grove across the street, and listened more closely for the whisper. But she had become quiet.

That evening, I attended a reception before the Aspen Ideas Festival began and found Laurene to give her a brief update on the fast-moving medical news.

"Did you say fifteen centimeters?" Laurene asked.

"Yes," I said. "I mean—I feel okay. But this fever is worrisome. I think it's best if I head home early."

"Agreed. Get to Stanford. Keep me posted." We shared a knowing look. She knew about livers and lab tests—more than anyone in my life—and I could tell by her face, which showed a combination of steady calm and steady seriousness, that the season of me assuming this would all blow over was drawing to a close.

Laurene encouraged me to fly home as quickly as possible, and by the time I landed, my fever was spiking again. There was now heightened concern the suspected abscess might erupt, so I had just enough time to race to my house, pack a bag, and go to the Stanford ER. An infectious-disease team was waiting for me, and I was ushered into a secure room with carefully draped nurses moving in and out to take my vitals. What's more, it was entirely unclear then as to whether I was infectious, so the ER team took every precaution to isolate me once I arrived. A CT scan was ordered to better understand the mass on my liver, and then I was wheeled back to my isolation room.

My friend Patti joined me about an hour later. She and I had met just weeks after the kids and I had gotten settled into our new neighborhood in Menlo Park; Lucy and Patti's daughter, Emily, had become fast first-day-of-third-grade friends and it didn't take them long to connect their moms to sort out playdates and sleepovers.

Early on, Lucy had announced to Emily that her parents were getting divorced and that her dad lived close to Disneyland, and how about that? Here's what's remarkable about Patti: she found me—within, what? hours—and suggested we have coffee.

I thought she was interested in getting better acquainted with Emily's new friend's mom, a time to make sure I didn't have a pentagram tattoo. Instead, Patti did the brave thing: she named the insanity. "So, you and your kids just moved here, and now you're getting divorced? A new job too? This is a lot. I wonder if I might ever be able to help." And *then* she did the most uncommon thing of all: she named how she might help. School pickups, tips on dentists in the area, how to get connected to the local tennis ladies.

Patti was also a retired pediatrician. Is there any better angel on the planet for a newly created single mom? It's one thing to meet an angel, it's quite another to have one with an MD behind her name show up for you, again and again.

And now here she was, in my triage room. We talked about best-case scenarios—*Well, if it's an abscess, I'm happy to help with the kids for the next couple of days*—and whispered about the worst case.

Dr. Jones didn't return. Instead, a new group of physicians came by to say that the CT scan revealed that the mass was suspicious enough that it was important for me to be admitted until a biopsy could be performed. And there it was: *biopsy.* The door to the next room of my life—foreboding and uncertain—edged ominously open a crack.

The next day, I had the biopsy. I was told that if this was an infection, the surgeon might be able to tell. I was semiawake during the procedure and looked the surgeon in the eye. "So, maybe it's not a tumor, right?"

He looked at me with somber eyes. "It has all the properties of a tumor. But you won't know for sure until you get these lab results back." Then, "I'm sorry."

I was alone that night in the hospital, still not sure what, or who, to tell.

Sebastien texted:

Sebastien: Are you up for a visitor? I'm happy to come down.

Me: Oh it's 9:00pm and you're all the way up in the city.

Sebastien: It's no trouble. I'll be there in about 45 minutes.

I looked for my cosmetic bag to put on lipstick and frantically searched for anything to wear other than my bad sweatshirt. I had luck with the lipstick, but no luck on the sweatshirt.

Sebastien arrived to my dimly lit room. His remarkable smile and chocolate-brown eyes brought a light I had been desperate for all those hours alone staring at a dark ceiling hearing my elderly roommate struggle with her sleep.

We walked out to the lounge area, and I took a seat on a couch, thinking that just days prior we'd been on his couch, and we were quite good together on couches.

But he didn't sit next to me. Instead, he found a chair and brought it over and sat directly across from me. He was just three feet away, but in that moment, it was more like miles.

In the last year of my marriage, I'd developed an extraordinarily perceptive eye. I could spot microscopic moments and understand them for what they were: shifts.

And so, I knew. Our nascent story was turning.

With the taking of the chair and the sitting across, our new romance shifted, unequivocally. Sebastien was now my friend who happened to be a doctor. We spoke of the usual things that two people speak of in a hospital lobby while waiting for biopsy results who just days earlier were intimately tangled up on a couch in front of a fireplace: nothing, and everything.

My fever spiked again that weekend while we were in waiting mode. I knew the results would come soon, so I lined up my brother and sister to be on standby so we could hear the news together.

But then, a knock on my hospital-room door. In walked Dr. Chen, a hospitalist, which is to say a smart generalist who is often on the front lines of delivering news. He entered carrying a mobile folding chair, a device I'd spotted for the first time just ten days earlier at the US Open in Pebble Beach. Older spectators had unfolded these little contraptions to watch putts and save their backs. I swear he pulled that strange little apparatus out of his white doctor's coat.

Dr. Chen perched and then began.

"Well, I'm afraid I have tough news, and I assume it will come as a kick in the shins. The results of your biopsy are in. You have stage IV colon cancer, and it's spread to your liver. It's a hard diagnosis. I'm sorry."

There was more. It was a blur of words about oncology and colonoscopies and the odds and getting me to specialists, but what I remember most was his little collapsible chair. That stupid, smug, ridiculous little three-legged contraption. Did he carry it everywhere? Did his kids beg him not to bring it to weekend soccer matches? Did he brag about it in the breakroom?

He delivered his words with great care, but I hated each one. They were awful, and the notion of shooting the messenger started to resonate with me like never before.

When he left, I realized I'd forgotten to put anyone else on speaker phone to catch the nuance—if there was nuance—of the news. But there was only one person to call. Only two people mattered: Connor and Lucy. The lights on the stage went dim, and the two of them were sitting under spotlights. As I looked at my life's stage in my mind's eye, Don walked back to the center from the wings. The years of Don being a ghost to me ended in one phone call.

"Don," I said in a whisper. "I have news. And it's not good. Are you in a place where you can talk?" He had flown back up that morning, both of us bracing for the biopsy news.

"I'm just pulling into your house. I'll call you back when I'm not in the car."

The phone rang three minutes later. He was in my bedroom.

"Okay," I said. "It's not good. I have stage IV colon cancer. And the doctor who was in my room said my odds weren't great. We need to sort out how to tell Connor and Lucy."

What I heard next was a mix of raw tears, regret, apologies, and chaos. "Oh, Amy. No. I caused this. Do you think I caused this? It's not right. I should have been the one to get cancer. This isn't right." He gasped. He whispered, "I'm so sorry."

And then, "Can I do this with you? What I mean is, do you have anyone in your life that you want to do this with? If not, I want to be that person. If you'll let me."

I stared at the ceiling, wishing beyond every wish I'd ever wished that I had someone in my life to do this with.

But after six solid years of recovery and rebuilding—and dating and all the glorious highs and lows of living through good but not forever romantic relationships—at that moment, I had to face the harsh reality that, no, there was no one close enough to be my partner for the hardest trek of all.

What I had was an ex-husband crippled by guilt and regret, and still good, reaching out to be that person. What I had were two teenagers who could very well be on the verge of losing their mom.

If Don was walking back to center stage with a starring role in whatever act of this life I was now moving through, I knew I had to wrestle with my heart's unfinished work. I hadn't fully forgiven Don and had instead found an unusual ease around it. Can you even forgive a ghost? Suspension seemed like a simpler path. Don remained fully alive and devoted as a dad, and the kids had the best of him. I thought my heart would eventually move on to full reconciliation. Except now I was being told there would no longer be a moving on. There would only be a drawing to a close.

It was my first glimpse of the last room. I wasn't sure where to sit.

Minutes after Dr. Chen collapsed his hobbit chair and walked out of my room, and after I had my chaotic call with Don, I had my brother, sister, and sister-in-law on the phone for an impromptu sibling conference. But before I assembled the sibs, I texted Sebastien:

> Biopsy results are in. I suppose it's the worst-case scenario. Stage IV colon cancer but apparently it's cancer in my liver, and I still don't understand that part.

His reply:

> Yes. I know. I can call you in a little while but know that in about 20 minutes a surgeon is going to be in your room. His name is Brendan Visser and he'll explain this to you. Stay hopeful. He'll explain.

My mind danced among *How would Sebastien already know?* and *How would he know which doctor was going to enter my room?* and *Why does everyone keep calling this colon cancer when it's in my liver?*

My call with my siblings was a standard mix of shock and pivots to who's telling Mom and Dad and who might be able to fly to help me first. We all knew Don was back in the mix, but it was far too soon to have a point of view about that new and deeply awkward dynamic. All we knew was to check flights and assume battle stations. I was in the middle of explaining that Menlo Park was actually right in between the San Jose and San Francisco airports, so either airport would work, when a new doctor entered my room in scrubs.

"Uh, guys? I have to go. I'll call you back."

"Hi, there. Amy Low? I'm Brendan Visser. I believe we have a friend in common—we seem to both know Sebastien. He's one of the best."

I was staring at him, puzzling over the idea of whether there was a land in between *was* and *is*, when he said again, "Amy? Hi. I'm Dr. Visser."

"Yes, Sebastien mentioned you might stop by. I've already gotten the awful news, so don't worry—you don't have to drop the bomb here. The deed has been done. Also—can you clear up how it is that I have colon cancer, but, apparently, it's really liver cancer?"

"Let's first take a step back here. I want you to know that this is a serious diagnosis, and I'm sorry. But I also want you to know something else: There's a playbook for this. And it works. You're going to have several rounds of chemo. It's not fun, but you'll handle it well. You're young. Other than the stage IV colon part, you seem healthy. So, you'll have these rounds of chemo. And then we'll scan again, and that fifteen-centimeter tumor on your liver is going to shrink. And then you'll do a colonoscopy to sort out what's going on in your colon. Once we know that, I'll operate on you and remove what's left of the cancer in your abdomen. Then you'll do a few more rounds of chemo to bolt the door shut. And that's how this is going to work."

"Wait, but Dr. Chen—he had this chair—he told me I would need a colonoscopy, like, tomorrow, I think."

"Yeah, no. That's not happening. I've ordered a chemo line into you as early as tomorrow. We're starting now. Whatever is in your colon we'll sort out later."

"Okay. But back to this liver situation. How is it that I don't have liver cancer?"

"We know from the biopsy. Colon cancer typically travels from colon to liver to lung. For you, this cancer chose to grow one very large tumor on your liver. And, oddly, that's something in your favor—surgeons aren't afraid of size. What we dread are scattered, smaller mets."

"A met?"

"A metastasis."

"Ah. Okay. A met."

"Oh, and speaking of the lungs, there's one important thing we're going to do before we start you on chemo. We need to do a CT scan to see if there's any activity in your lungs. Oh, and that brings us back to Sebastien. He's one of the best surgeons in the nation. You're fortunate to know him. He found me immediately to give me a heads-up on your case, so I'm glad I was able to stop in today."

My eyes welled up with the enormity of all that I was hearing alongside the crushing memory of the lobby and Sebastien's chair maneuver. I was sorting out what to mourn, and in which order, when I drifted back to the conversation at hand. "Okay. But wait, what if there are—mets?—in my lungs?"

"We'll see what we find. If there are, we'll probably follow the same playbook. Your chemo is called FOLFOX, and you won't lose your hair. It will thin some, but it's not too bad. You'll even do most of your treatments at home."

"Did you say Firefox? My chemo is called Firefox?"

"No. FOLFOX. You'll also need an excellent oncologist, so I'm recommending you to Dr. Natalia Colocci, who's with Palo Alto Medical Foundation. So, she's close."

"Oh, okay. So, not someone here at Stanford?"

"You could have an oncologist from Stanford, but I'm concerned you'll be assigned to someone who may spend more time delivering papers at conferences and less time seeing you. Natalia is as good as they come, and she's patient-centered."

"Okay. Thanks." An Italian oncologist. I remembered then that my third date with Don was a weekend in Italy, and it might have been the most marvelous seventy-two hours of my life.

I was running my fingers through my hair and thinking about how bananas it was that when I was twenty-eight I could fly to Italy for a weekend, when Dr. Visser glanced at his watch. "I need to leave now. I'll check on you before you're discharged."

"Yes, okay. Thank you for the playbook. The good news here is that—as it turns out—I'm horribly free this week, so I say let's just get started."

He smiled, a smile so warm it could heat the coldest wind of fear ripping through my veins. He exited the room, and I glanced at my phone.

My mom had called. And Don had texted. He was on his way over to the hospital.

Noble, adj. Having or showing fine personal qualities or high moral principles and ideals.

So, this word *noble*. Paul lists it second among his virtues, the lanterns for my last room. Some translations of Paul's letter to his beloveds in Philippi swap *honorable* for *noble*. Both words label graceful attributes but aren't ones we often use to describe our lives, or the lives of those who saunter onto the stage of our life's play.

When I first began to illuminate my last room with Paul's virtues, I thought *noble* was elegant but a bit set apart from the others. Nobility struck me as exquisitely aspirational, a lofty ideal meant to raise expectations for heroic outcomes. But lofty ideals have a way of arriving as a package deal with hall passes for the inevitable and ignoble decisions that clutter our days. We strive, we stumble. We learn. I logged *noble* as part of the striving part of the equation; I related far more to the stumbling.

Besides, this last room was a stage-four-alarm fire, and the very notion of reaching for *noble* began to strike me as absurd. What on earth was Paul thinking tucking this word among his greatest hits? The more I turned this word over in my mind, the more elitist it sounded. *Noble* is precious. I was struggling to keep up with thank-you texts and needed permission to be pathetic instead of an admonition to fly at some impossibly high altitude of nobility.

I let *noble* go.

So *noble* decided to find me instead. February 2022. A quiet evening. I was doing what anyone with time on their hands might have been doing back in February 2022: doom scrolling about Ukraine or the pandemic, and in my case, both.

But there in my Twitter feed, a magical thread appeared. A physician was posting some helpful insights for fellow physicians, but this time from the point of view of a daughter of a patient. She had been caring for her elderly mother in the hospital and decided it was time to relay some pragmatic words of wisdom to clinicians busy on rounds.

She had a smart set of reminders: explain plans for discharge in plain English, both to the patient and to their caregiver; speak loudly because we're all wearing masks in the hospital these days;

describe in better detail how medications patients are taking home will work.

And she wrote this: "Invest in something called the Rounding with a Purpose Stool." A collapsible little chair, where you can sit and look into the eyes of your patient when you deliver important news.

She concluded her thread by simply saying, "Take time to listen." While sitting on the little stool. At eye level. With your patient.

Oh, Dr. Chen. Did you have that little stool in the trunk of your car? And did you read my chart and hustle all the way out to your car before entering my room? Or was it in your locker, where you stow your workout clothes? Or did you maybe borrow it from another doctor?

All I know is that you had it with you. On purpose. Because you knew that you were the one summoned to tell me the most awful news, and you knew how important it would be to look into my eyes rather than stand and hover over my bed, with a terrible hierarchy of height that would confuse rather than console.

You did your absolute best, and you brought your fabulous, adorable, practically made-for-preschoolers chair. You relayed this horrific news in the most noble way possible. By sitting next to me, at my level, and holding my gaze throughout.

You saw me tear up, and you heard me talk about my kids and how they were way too young to lose their mom. How they might be so scared, and how would it work if I wasn't around to comfort them?

You let me talk about the letters. I asked you how much time I might have left because I needed to write letters to Connor and

Lucy. I had been writing them a letter for their birthday every year, and there was still so much more to say. I was ticking through the letters I would have to write while you sat there on your perch, quiet, listening. How Lucy should think about finding roommates after college and how to sort out when and where to wear red lipstick, encouragements for Connor for whenever he might become a dad. Plus fifty thousand other topics.

And you sat there, on your chair, staying present.

I suspect Dr. Chen knew then that there's no time more vulnerable than when you discover that you're sick, especially when you feel more or less well. And if you're the one delivering that news, there's nothing more noble than bringing as much empathy, compassion, and humanity—and eye-level eye contact—as you can offer.

I suspect Dr. Chen knew something else. Nobility at first blush seems rarefied. Or about position. A person is born into nobility. But are they? Nobility has an aura—a space where the ceremonial is consecrated with intentionality.

Dr. Chen showed me that to be noble is to be a certain kind of person. And it's open to anyone—regardless of their position, or their status—who chooses to create a holy space. When that space is created, it endures. The very act of living this virtue means an ordinary moment becomes majestically sacred, even if it's heartbreaking.

Dr. Chen and his miraculous teeny, tiny chair guided me to one of the most hallowed corners of my last room: the space that says, *Come, it's time, be here, come closer to the fragility of life, and be brave.* This is a noble place.

Whatever Is Right

I'VE OFTEN SAID TO CLOSE FRIENDS—PROBABLY TOO CASUALLY—that divorce is harder than cancer. Here is what I mean.

It was far more crushing to hold Connor's and Lucy's hands and walk them into the new country called Divorce than it was to beckon them over to a new realm called Cancer. With cancer, I told them, "Here is the lousy news and this is why I've been so tired lately.

"But do you see this bag of liquid hanging up here connected to my arm? This bag of clear liquid is a miracle—a hard miracle. I'm going to feel like crap while I take it and it's going to be a slog. But this is *not* poison, despite what you might hear some say. No. This liquid is going to save my life, and it's dripping into my arm because for decades people studied, worked hard, and studied again to make it as safe and effective as possible. There's simply nothing poisonous about that."

Unlike the divorce, decades of brilliant minds and magnificent science had been focused on this very moment. Their work—their gift—emerged as a path. And although uncertain, the path came with a map my kids and I could follow.

Because the divorce was uniquely our own, we had stumbled through those early days in uncharted territory. Like all families going through divorce, our story belonged only to us, forcing us into an inevitable season of internal reckoning and repair—a time that occasionally required a kind of brutal isolation. We were fortunate to have a community of family, new friends, and longtime soulmates who offered generous love through those days, but at its core, binding up the wounds of a family happens quietly within its interior life. If the campaign in those days was to emerge from the valley of despair into a new place—a place where our hearts would once again be dependably joyful and open—were we advancing at an appropriate pace? How would we know?

Divorce had no clinical trials pointing the way to the most efficient or effective route to recovery. Divorce had no published reports that would help me know whether I ought to have insisted that Don fly up for a parent-teacher conference. Divorce had no ninety-day scans to show whether the wounds of our hearts were healing without leaving too much scar tissue.

Then again, there was no chance I could die of divorce.

Dr. Visser said colon cancer typically travels from the colon to the liver and then to the lungs. Colon, liver, lung. A trail, likely ancient, where billions of cells within millions of individuals have mistakenly beat a path to dire outcomes.

When I was diagnosed, Visser ordered a full CT scan to see if my lungs had been touched by the madness. There was such a mix of adrenaline and chaos in those early hours that I nearly missed the nuance of how Visser and his squad of residents—always two steps behind him—delivered the findings.

They'd entered my room, a new private one where I could safely be administered my first round of chemotherapy. Usually, patients receive chemotherapy in outpatient units, but I needed to stay in the hospital for continued surveillance and there was no time to lose given the size of the tumor on my liver.

Instead of scrubs, this time Visser arrived dressed in the most handsome suit. Dark olive, with a light-blue shirt and corresponding tie with bold diagonal navy stripes. "You're on your way here with this first round of FOLFOX. Your fevers will most likely stop now—your immune system has been putting up a valiant fight for a long time, but now the cavalry is coming in the form of what's in the IV bag, so keep that in mind through these next cycles."

"Yes, I've decided to call the chemo Foxy," I said, glancing up at the clear fluids dripping into my IV. "Her aim will be strong and true."

Visser smiled. "Now for the lungs. We saw a little activity, but it's hard to tell exactly what's there. A few schmaltzies here and there. All very small. Any chance you grew up in an area with a lot of air pollution?"

When I was a kid, we used to brag how San Diego was not Los Angeles, how most days the skies were a perfect blue. "Not really, no," I answered.

"Right. Well, even if the schmaltzies are small mets, this doesn't change the playbook. FOLFOX will address those too. You'll be discharged tomorrow, and you should have your port put in by Monday for future infusions. You and I will connect again in a few months to sort out the next play."

The adrenaline in those earliest hours ushered in hope. Waves of optimism that would lift me up to new heights of joy as I fell in love with the power and miracle of Visser's playbook. And just as Visser had predicted, my persistent fever stopped within hours of Foxy pulsing through my veins. I was in awe.

But adrenaline was fleeting, a rush of intoxicating hope followed by a hard reckoning that came when I summoned the courage to behold the gravity of my situation. That night I sobbed—gasping cries, the kind that don't resolve—through the heaviness of watching Foxy drip into my arm in a dark and lonely hospital room. The solitude and utter unfairness of it all were unbearable. I grieved all the milestones I would likely miss. I'd miss hearing Lucy describe to me how she negotiated for a raise at work someday. Connor might score the soundtrack to a film in 2038, and I'd miss the screening. But what I was grieving most was the heavy realization that I would have to surrender the magical mundane in my future. Those moments that float in, the ones that create a soft pause, and that forge a lifetime of companionship between a mom and her kids.

Like many parents who travel for work, when the kids were young I would often fly home from a trip bearing small toys or tokens from the city I'd been visiting—a well-intended habit that resulted in clutter that grew with each trip. One day, after purging an assortment of snow globes and untouched coloring books, I realized that I could be more intentional about bringing home stories from my travels rather than trinkets.

The year before I got sick, I was in Washington, DC, spending time with nonprofit journalism newsrooms, a grantmaking portfolio I helped develop with Emerson. Part of this trip included a day with lawmakers and other legal experts that had been organized by The Marshall Project, a newsroom that reports solely on the US legal and criminal justice systems. The day concluded after a conversation with Adam Liptak from the *New York Times*, who previewed the Supreme Court's upcoming docket and possible decisions in the months to come. He took particular care in walking us through the possible implications of *Masterpiece Cakeshop v. Colorado Civil Rights Commission*, a case that proved to be a precursor to *303 Creative LLC v. Elenis*, the ruling that said that the State of Colorado could not compel a website designer to create work if it was in tension with her personal values. The ruling was considered a win for free speech and religious-freedom advocates and a painful setback for LGBTQ rights.

The night I got home, Lucy, Connor, and I settled into dinner and—in keeping with the soft promise I'd made myself earlier—I gave them a crisp summary of Liptak's take on the cakebaker case. Within about two minutes, both kids declared an identical opinion on my summary: "Well, this case is a no-brainer."

"Mom, it's so obvious. Of course the court has to rule for the gay couple getting married," Lucy said.

Connor sat up straighter. "Wait, what? The court can't tell an artist what to do. I'm a musician. Could the law someday tell me I have to play in a venue that I—for whatever reason—don't support?"

They both looked at each other in disbelief, stunned that they'd reached opposite conclusions from my admittedly shallow summary of the matter at hand. There was little nuance or careful listening at the dinner table that night; base-level adolescent biases about the long-standing tension between free speech and protections to guard against discrimination were in abundance.

As the two of them engaged in a spirited debate, the marvelous mundane materialized. I listened to them communicate their teenage convictions, fascinated that they'd landed on opposite sides. As I cleaned the kitchen that night, I wondered if their differing vantage points were a by-product of my affinity for being a bridge dweller—do you end up giving birth to mini versions of Elena Kagan and Neil Gorsuch?

Later, months after my diagnosis, I thought of that discussion and wondered whether in eighteen years a thirty-four-year-old Connor and a thirty-two-year-old Lucy would stay true to their opening bids in that discussion, or whether a friendship or a summer job or a novel might shift their view.

I would likely never find out. One of millions of moments in my future I was finding a way to release.

I finished my first round of Foxy on a Friday, capping off five days in the Stanford hospital: a dizzying spin from diagnosis to starting

Visser's playbook to sharing the news with Connor and Lucy to Foxy's arrival and, finally, to discharge. I was eager to leave; Stanford's hospital staff provided world-class care, but the building felt suffocating. I overheard many of the nurses small-talk about the new hospital building, now nearly complete and just a hundred or so yards away, and how everyone's life—patients and staff—would be upgraded soon.

Given the chaos—and the understandable fear the kids were beginning to move through—I accepted that Don was the appropriate person to be on point for me at home. The kids needed their dad close, and I knew I would, too, if I were to take another turn for the worse. At least for the handful of days ahead, I thought it made sense for Don to be with us at the house. He wanted very much to help. I would be sleeping far more than usual, and he also knew me so very well; we still shared all those instincts a couple creates over years of shorthand language.

Remember that place in Seattle with that pasta . . . ?

Yes, I can make it for you . . .

For the handful of days ahead, it made sense for Don to bridge me over to my friends as we all found our footing.

The notion of "what is right" occupies numerous realms. We use the same word—*right*—to describe a cake recipe as we do a local mayoral candidate. *Yes, you have all the right ingredients. Yes, she's obviously the right choice for our town.*

The word itself is vague enough, context-dependent enough, subjective enough, and maddeningly ambiguous enough—it was tempting to view Paul's idea of "right" as an easy reminder to simply show up to my doctors' appointments on time. While I worked through this question about whether it was "right" for Don to care for me at home—to move back into his earlier role, even with all the unresolved wounds—I came to see that there was a richer set of insights that I might gain from this virtue and a broader understanding of Paul's intention in including it in the list.

Of Paul's virtues, *right* has become my primary source of illumination in my room. The Greek word Paul uses for *right* is *dikiaos*, which translates closer to "righteous," and it's why some biblical translations use the word *just* in this verse. In this context, Paul is inviting me to embrace a wider view of how to incorporate this word into a lamp for my last room.

He is asking me to set aside the notion of *right* as a synonym for *correct* and instead to welcome the word as the act of putting a decision in motion toward what is good. This aiming toward what is right requires a purposeful outlook, which in turn requires sacrifice, trust, faith, and dedicated patience, for it's a long-term endeavor.

The kind of *right* Paul includes in his list of virtues is not rule-based. Rather, it's a type of discernment that folds in all the people and circumstances surrounding a decision and purposefully embraces a bias toward betterment.

Even though I was still finding my footing with folding Don back into my life, I knew the days ahead might teach me something new; the light I was coming to better understand might show me an unexpected discovery in the room and perhaps set something better in motion.

As I was waiting outside for Don to pull up in the car to take me home from the hospital, I texted Sebastien to thank him for the remarkable help, to let him know that I was finally headed home and that I was now embarking on this mountain climb in earnest. I also gave him full permission to exit this chaotic story with as much grace and gratitude as I could convey.

We had met only two months earlier, and though we'd enjoyed a few lovely dates and seemed to find a sweet spark, this insanity was no place for anyone to feel awkwardly obligated.

Instead of texting back, Sebastien called while I was still waiting for Don, standing in the Stanford summer sun.

"Oh, hi," I answered.

"Hi, there," he said. "Hey, I just read your text. I know we don't know each other all that well and thanks for the offer to exit, but I won't be going anywhere. I want to be helpful in any way I can, so know that I'll stay as close here as you'd like."

His call was endearing and perfectly appropriate. Generous, but not overly so. Full of heart, but careful too. We exchanged more pleasantries, and I hung up before I climbed into the passenger seat. I wondered if this was the beginning of a friendship for which I had no frame of reference—cancer support pal who also happens to be a ridiculously handsome surgeon who had a special talent for reading scans?

I glanced at Don and realized I needed to find a frame of reference for him, too. My ex-husband, father to my children, and the one who seemed more crushed than any of us by the news that Dr. Chen on his little chair had delivered.

For many cancer patients, the first big medical appointment begins with a relatively simple surgery to have something called a port inserted underneath your skin, near your collarbone. It's a device about the size of a quarter that is the main gateway for all manner of nurses and lab techs to either draw blood or infuse life-saving drugs. Instead of finding a vein in your arm, a nurse can simply access your little port and insert a much smaller needle in much less time.

I was told to come back to Stanford the following Monday to have my port inserted, a procedure that would involve some pre-op prep, so it was important that I have someone drive me to the hospital and back home.

By this point, the obvious conversations and instincts had begun. I googled my cancer using a more precise set of search terms and then implored anyone close to me to maybe not google so much.

So, instead, I forced myself to focus on Dr. Visser's playbook. My port procedure was slated for 9:00 a.m. Don insisted on driving, and my sister-in-law, Julie, had flown in from Phoenix as additional support for whatever the days ahead were going to bring.

We were all running on a preposterous combination of grief, hope, determination, and exhaustion when we arrived at the check-in area to a new pile of paperwork. Don funneled his nervous energy into the forms—date, patient name, birthday, insurance, employer, allergies. Person responsible for driving the patient: Don Low. Relationship to patient: Husband.

Wait. Did I have cancer or amnesia?

I sauntered over to Julie and found a spot next to her on the couch. In my best ventriloquist's whisper, I managed, "Umm. He just said he was my husband on the form."

Julie put down her phone and murmured back, "Yeah. I think he called himself that at the hospital, too."

Sitting next to Julie, I processed Don's gesture for a moment. I found it both touching and unnerving: I hadn't actually seen Don in person for more than a few minutes at a time in at least five years, and yet the previous forty-eight hours of extreme adversity had catapulted us back into the parts of our marriage that had once been beautiful, full of trust and care. As I considered what felt like a contradiction, a nurse called my name and held open the door to the pre-op area.

My nurse Bridget led me down the hallway and had me climb onto one of the many beds separated by thin curtains so she could explain what's what. She scanned my chart, and her face dropped slightly. I had rapidly become accustomed to the face slump and how quickly most medical folks could rebound for the task at hand. "I know this is still quite a shock, but this part is fairly painless. All of this is hard, but these ports really do make it far easier to move through it all. We start by giving you some drugs to relax you—during the procedure you'll actually be a little bit awake so the surgeon can speak to you. But don't worry, you won't feel a thing."

"Why would the surgeon need to chat with me?"

"What? Oh. Well, it's more about not needing to put you all the way under."

"Oh, I'm fine to go all the way under. Let's just do that."

"Uh, huh. Well, yeah, no. We like to keep you awake so the surgeon can talk to you."

"About what?"

"You know what? I'm going to start your IV with these relaxing drugs and I'll be back in a few minutes. And, oh, hey—when our patients come back here to have their ports removed when all of their cancer is gone, we like to have what we call port parties. Amazing celebrations. Just think about that."

As rafts of soft clouds wafted around my bed, I thought about a theme for the port party I would have. I settled on Mexican, for no particular reason except that at that moment I was craving a margarita. The drugs were clearly kicking in.

Bridget returned to check on me.

"Hi, Bridget! All good here. How are you?"

"Okay, looks like those drugs are working. So, when you're done in surgery, you'll be delivered to a post-op area. A different team of nurses will be there. But don't worry, your husband will be there to greet you in Recovery."

"Wait, who?"

"Your husband."

"Bridget. I don't have a husband."

Bridget glanced at the forms and smiled. Her voice softened. "Oh, Amy, I know. This is such an awful time. I can only imagine the stress. But know that your husband is here, and he'll be by your side the minute you're done with surgery."

"Bridge," I whispered. "You need to come closer. I need to tell you something."

She was so close her badge was nearly touching my face.

"The man who drove me here and who will meet me after I get done small-talking with my surgeon? *That* man is quite lovely and often so very kind, but he decided to not be my husband a few years ago. And now he's back, Bridge. He's back and he's filling out forms and looking after our children and he's crying quite a bit and all of that is surprisingly touching, but hear me when I say that he is not. My. Husband."

Bridget tried to back away and glanced at my IV. "Okay. Got it. I'm just glad you have a driver. Drivers come in lots of shapes and sizes."

"Oh, and Bridge?"

But I was already being wheeled away before I could ask her about the mariachi band.

Sebastien's offer to stay connected proved to be genuine, and we found time for strolls and tea in-between my early Foxy rounds. I liked to keep him updated on how I was progressing through the playbook, in part because a soft nod or affirmation from him signaled that he might agree with my assessment of the situation. But unlike the rest of my friends, who would happily share in my optimism, a nod from Sebastien was a positive signal from a doctor, a doctor who had a deep familiarity with my case. I wondered if he knew that I would sometimes tee up this small talk to steer him toward any manner of casual proclamations: "You seem to be doing so well" or "Yes, your latest labs show some good hints the chemo is working" were pieces of gold in our long talks that I would tuck into my pocket.

Early that fall of 2019, I was chattering on about how I saw the playbook unfolding for the months ahead. I offered up my most optimistic prognosis, hoping he might concur. "So, I'll have a scan sometime the end of October, and if all goes as planned, I'll have surgery a few weeks after that, and then maybe a few more rounds of chemo for final button-up—"

"Mm-hmm," he mused. "Probably you'll have a little lung cleanup, though."

"Lung cleanup? You mean the schmaltzies that Visser mentioned? Oh, I'm not worried about that. He said Foxy would knock them out, so that's probably okay."

"Yeah. Maybe. We'll just have to see."

That "maybe" was the first of several calls Sebastien would get right.

By early November, I'd completed nine rounds of Foxy, and though I liked to note to my friends and work colleagues that I was handling it all like a champ, those closest to me knew I was exhausted. And the side effects I'd shrugged off in the earlier rounds were circling like sharks in the water, swimming ever closer.

Lucy and I had become fans of *Stranger Things* and she would occasionally glance at me and swipe at her nose—our code for letting me know my nose was bleeding like Eleven. At the beginning, we could laugh about it. But by November, we were over it.

My hands and feet were also feeling the effects of the neuropathy I'd been warned so much about. Cold was usually a trigger, so opening the refrigerator resulted in my hands cramping so that I couldn't hold anything. For weeks, we kept bottles of vitamin water on the counter—room temperature—each with their tops carefully unscrewed. Fine motor skills also became a challenge. Anything that required an intricate finger turn was usually a disaster. I would often wander into Lucy's room at night and ask her to unclasp a necklace or remove my earrings. I remember thinking that if I'd been a professional knitter, my career would have come to a screeching halt.

My November scan to determine next steps was scheduled for an early morning on a Monday. This was only my third scan, so I wasn't quite sure how the results would be communicated to me.

Dr. Colocci called midday. "There's been modest improvement. We'll discuss at our appointment tomorrow."

"Okay. Improvement seems encouraging."

"Yes. As I said, it's modest. We'll discuss tomorrow at our appointment."

Dr. Colocci is a remarkably talented oncologist. Degrees from the most prestigious of institutions hang on her exam-room walls, and she was fiercely present at every appointment. She was current on the data, attended to every detail, and brought her full self to every question I raised. The nurses held her in the highest regard, which I thought was such a beautiful badge of honor. But like a laser-sharp umpire, she called it like she saw it, with zero interest in spin.

Don had flown up to be with me for the scan and to spend time with the kids after several weeks away. He came to the appointment with me, and I was still struggling to know how to introduce him.

Dr. Colocci entered the room, smiled, and took her seat.

"Hi, there," I said. "This is . . . Don. He's here this time."

I'd had so many friends join me for different chemo rounds and follow-up appointments with Dr. Colocci that I'd forgotten whether she'd met him before. She had. "Hi. Nice to see you again." Then we got down to business.

She showed me the images of my liver, carefully pointing out the tumor. It had certainly shrunk—down from roughly fifteen centimeters to about seven centimeters—but it was still formidable.

Dr. Colocci looked at me clear-eyed. "It's still quite large. I'm not sure you'll be a candidate for surgery."

The wind went out of me.

"But I thought this was the next step. What's the alternative?"

Dr. Colocci glanced down at her cute shoes and then looked up at me with a mix of compassion and clarity. "We can try more chemo."

"Right, but what does that get me? The only path forward is to remove the tumor, correct? I guess what I'm asking is, what project are we working on here?"

"I'm trying to get you more time."

Then I looked at my shoes. Black pumps. Wide heels that were both fashionable and more comfortable. I was dressed for an important conference I was set to attend in San Francisco later that afternoon and decided I wanted to walk in not looking like a cancer patient.

As clearly as I could, I asked about what might be next. Dr. Colocci could see the tears welling in my eyes.

"You should have Dr. Visser look at the scans. He may see a way here, and ultimately this will be his call. You'll need to see him soon, though."

Miraculously, I was able to get a Friday appointment with Dr. Visser to see if he could find a future that Dr. Colocci hinted he might see. In the meantime, I had the images on my phone. I texted them to Sebastien, praying his surgeon's eye might open a door to a new and more hopeful trail up this forever-high mountain.

I drove to San Francisco considering how I could attend a conference and take thoughtful notes and make small talk with colleagues while at the same time wondering if I had only a few weeks left to live.

Sebastien called as I listened to a panel discussion. I slipped out to the lobby.

"Hi. I know this is bananas, but I wonder if you're able to look at these pictures and see if I might be a candidate for surgery?"

"Yes, hi. I got your texts. I'm in meetings, but let's plan to talk in a couple of hours. But at first glance, I think there might be a path. Let's talk later."

I walked back to my seat and gathered my things, surrendering to the reality that I was only physically present, and slipped outside. I found a bench in a courtyard and began calling anyone who would pick up.

My friend Jacquelline answered. She heard the fear in my voice and kept me on the line, patiently asking about the process, the pragmatics, and the pathways. She's my gorgeous left-brain friend; her logic comes in handy when what you want most of all is someone to hold your hand as you stumble in the fog. She then asked the best and bravest question of all.

"Okay," Jacquelline said. "What are you most afraid of?"

I inhaled, then gasped for breath. "I'm most afraid of leaving Connor and Lucy. It's too soon. I have too much I still want them to have from me."

Jacquelline was quiet. And then she said this. "All right. So that's the core fear. Here's my thought. If the news from Visser is awful, we should gather your closest girlfriends for a weekend retreat and we'll get an uninterrupted two days to hear what you want us to provide for Connor and Lucy. We'll be strategic about this. You'll have some of us focused on career, others on relationships, some on their faith. Do you have anyone who's good with fashion? We may need her there. We can start thinking about an agenda and I'll bring flip charts and let's go someplace beautiful and we'll map this out."

Thank God for the Left Brains. Those dazzling planners. Their embrace of practicality is the pair of outstretched arms ready to catch a dangling trapeze artist. They say: Trust, even if this means you might fall. We'll start sewing the net.

Sebastien called toward the end of the afternoon. After we went through all the requisite caveats—that he was seeing only a couple of images, that his specialty was lungs and that he was looking at a liver, and that he was looking at images taken with my phone when my hands were shaking—we got down to it.

"The tumor is smaller, that's for sure."

"Right, but is it small enough to remove?"

Throughout the previous four months and many rounds of chemo, I had become acquainted with friends of friends who were also living on Planet Stage IV Metastatic Colon Cancer. Most were my age or a little younger. We all had this liver issue in common. Each of them was many steps ahead of me and had sustained successful surgeries. I had learned a new phrase living on this planet, more of a mantra really: "No cut, no cure." I knew enough by November to know that if my story didn't follow Visser's playbook—chemo, surgery, chemo—this story would be coming to an abrupt end.

"You know surgeons aren't as concerned about size, actually," he said.

I remembered that Visser had said the same thing. But then, why did Dr. Colocci have misgivings? "So, you're more encouraged? You think there's a path here with surgery?"

He paused. And then took the conversation to a new place.

"You know," he said, "we're all mortal. I mean, I know you know this, but we're all going to die."

"Sebastien. Did you really just say that? You know I have two kids, right?"

"How old are Connor and Lucy, again?"

"Sixteen and fourteen."

"Right. Well, you know the bulk of raising them is done now. There's so much data on that. How the core work is behind you. You should feel so proud."

I knew Sebastien well enough by this point to know that in a place of ambiguity, he sprinted to clarity. Speculation, nuance, and hypotheticals could cause terrible harm when talking about pathways in an operating room. So, he was guiding me to the safest place he knew—data.

I realized then I had as much wisdom to give Sebastien as I was desperately trying to claw out of him. "You're lovely to take time out of your busy afternoon to help me process through this. And your science and data about human development and what we know of the frontal lobe and adolescent growth and the core work of parenting are—I'm sure—unequivocally sound. I'm not disputing that. That said, I wonder if I might suggest that you've missed the point here.

"I'm aware that Connor and Lucy are old enough to step into adulthood ready to flourish. But here's the thing. If I die in a few months, they'll miss me. They'll wake up for thousands of mornings and want to see me, and I won't be there. An agony will begin for them, and I won't be here to comfort them. It's not about their cognitive functions. It's about their hearts."

I paused, terrified. Then whispered, "This, Sebastien, is why I'm quite eager to know if Visser is going to operate."

Another pause.

"When are you meeting with Visser?"

"Friday."

"My best hunch here is that he's going to find a way to do this."

Friday morning I arrived at Visser's Stanford office exhausted. Why don't more people talk about sleep deprivation on Planet Cancer? It can't be good for us, and it's got to be the most common side effect of the uncertainty.

In the waiting area, I glanced around at the other patients. We were a classic cross section of Silicon Valley. I heard someone on the phone who sounded like she worked for a start-up; a couple who had driven up from Salinas who worked in the agricultural fields; an older gentleman wearing a Giants baseball jersey.

Some were more obviously hollowed out by treatments, and I was easily the youngest. But I was the only one quietly, and overtly, crying. Over the years, I had perfected the art of invisible crying—how many times had I wandered through a grocery store wearing sunglasses to mask my tears only to pivot to an easy smile at checkout?

Mainly because of my sleep deprivation, I wore my tears publicly this time. They were practically a T-shirt slogan: "This evening I'll be telling my teenagers that I have only a few weeks to live." Others in the waiting area exchanged glances with me and then turned away. We all knew sorrow was contagious, and no one wanted to catch my downward spiral.

In the exam room, Visser entered impeccably dressed in a light-gray suit trailed by his physician assistant. He took the small stool opposite me, pulled up my scan images, and swirled around to meet my eyes.

"You still have a sizable tumor here, but it's time to get this out."

"So, you see a way to operate?" Relief flooded all my chemo'd pathways. "How big is it, specifically, now?" The narrative report from the scan differed slightly from what Colocci had told me and I'd become fixated on this number.

"Have you ever tried to measure a cloud? Tumors can sometimes look larger or smaller based on how they shift around. What you need to know is I can get this out. Does this help clarify?"

"Yes," I said, amazed by such a clever analogy.

"And we need to do so soon. How many rounds of chemo have you had?"

"Nine. I'm tolerating it all very well," I said and began to give my brave speech about how I'm such a good soldier in the chemo department, but Visser cut me off.

"Right, okay. It's time to pause your treatments. You'll need about nine weeks off before I can operate, which will put us toward the third week of December for a surgery date. I'll meet with you again as we get closer. In the meantime, you'll need a colonoscopy to sort out the specifics of the original tumor, and from there we'll map out a plan for the surgery."

A week before surgery we reconvened for his time to walk me through how recovery would work.

"This is Cindy Kin," Dr. Visser said. "She'll be performing your upcoming surgery with me."

"Yes, hello," Dr. Kin said. "I'll be doing the resection on your colon, so I've gone through all the data from your recent colonoscopy." In the intervening weeks, I'd finally had the colonoscopy that pinpointed a medium-sized polyp tucked up in the left corner of my large intestine, next to my liver. At last, I learned why I hadn't had any traditional symptoms before my diagnosis. My cancer had hidden out until some of those destructive cells decided to pop over to my liver to live it up.

"Right," Dr. Visser continued. "This will be a significant abdominal surgery. I'll be resecting your liver, and I'll also be removing your gallbladder and spleen. Dr. Kin will handle the colon."

I was beginning to wonder if I would run out of body parts.

Visser was glancing at my latest scans while I peppered him with questions about my digestive system like I was back in the fourth grade—"So, what does a gallbladder really even do?"

He swiveled on his stool to look me more carefully in the eyes. He inhaled. It was as if the weight of my case was pushing his tailored shoulders down deep into his chest. "Look. You've come a long way and you've responded well to chemo. Your attitude is as positive as any patient I've had. And you're slim, so your recovery will be easier than some others'. But I want to be straight with you here. You have advanced disease. Cindy and I are going to do our part, but it's hard to know what we're going to find once we get going. I've seen cases much less severe than yours where patients died only a few months after surgery. And I've seen cases far more advanced than yours, and patients went on to live years. It's very hard to say. I just want you to understand we're now moving into a new phase here. You came in with extremely advanced disease, and we'll do our very best." He was delivering unvarnished truths and, like all excellent physicians, at the right time. Timing and dosage are as crucial in communicating with a patient as the medicines prescribed.

"I hear you. I appreciate the candor. And to recap one key point: You're saying I'm slim?"

They smiled and exited the room.

If you had to pick a bad day of the year for surgery, December 19 would rank up there. Connor and Lucy were in the thick of finals, my brother's and sister's families had important Christmas obligations, and my extended network of girlfriends had holiday plans and trips they'd booked months before.

I knew I would be well cared for in the hospital, but after comparing notes with a few others in my abdominal surgery club, I learned that the first days home would be painful, harrowing, and hampered by limited mobility.

Once the surgery date was set, my sister, Mindy, and Julie volunteered to come and be with the kids through my hospital days, but they both needed to get home in time for Christmas Eve. If all went well, I would likely be discharged by Christmas Day, and I'd need a caregiver on hand for those first highly vulnerable days.

Here's something most people find surprising about lots of us with cancer. Most days, we look normal. Each cancer and treatment is different, but many of us move in and out of chemo rounds and scans and procedures more or less looking like ourselves, at least most of the time.

I was passing for healthy while being gravely ill.

The schism between my insides and my outsides had proved immensely helpful while navigating those early months with Connor and Lucy. I took lots of naps and went to bed early. We ordered more pizza than normal, and I remember once saying the idea of unloading the dishwasher was just too much. But I still went to my office most days, took the kids to dentist appointments, attended school concerts, made breakfasts, carpooled, paid bills, and listened attentively to the latest gossip from their high school days.

In those days, the question I received more than any other was, "So, how are your kids holding up?" And my reply was always the same: "Most days are bizarrely normal, and they seem okay. Are they googling and rabbit-holing on the scary odds of stage IV colon cancer into the wee hours of the night? Maybe. But my theory here is that since I don't look sick, it's easier than you might think to not wake up every morning in a complete panic."

The days after the surgery would be different. I would look gaunt, sad, weak, shaky. My clever trick of living through an internal horror show while twirling around as if I were in a rom-com would come crashing down, and the kids would come not just to know but also *to see* the urgent reality: their mom was seriously ill.

So, when I wrestled with the dilemma of who would be best to be with me after discharge—the answer became obvious. It had to be Don. The kids would need their dad in those days when I would be at my most visibly vulnerable. Plus, it was Christmas, and I was desperate to give them some semblance of continuity as uncertainty persistently hovered over us.

This question of inviting Don back into my life—into the full uncertainty, intimacy, trust of our family—to care for me at my most defenseless was distinctly different from my earlier judgment call of allowing him to get me home from the hospital after the diagnosis and port procedure. That was more of a baton-pass call, a setting-aside-grievances-and-awkwardness kind of call.

These after-surgery days—I knew—would signal an important shift in me, a shift that probably no one else would fully observe, but one that would require every ounce of effort for me to embrace. A shift I was coming to think of as our marriage's third act.

As a practical matter, physical vulnerability would be ever present. I would need a steady arm to walk the eight paces to my bathroom, and God only knew what might happen in the bathroom after I got there. I would need help getting dressed and even getting in and out of the shower. And the pain. I'd been warned there would be late nights when I would cry out for help—and knowing that the person I would be crying out to would be Don felt humiliating.

But, ultimately, all that mattered were Connor and Lucy. If they were going to hear their mom cry out in agony in the middle of the night, I wanted them to hear me call for their dad.

After all those years living individually on the other side of marriage, they would witness their parents doing what they were always meant to do: carefully walking alongside each other. This, in a way that I initially struggled to grasp, could prove to be another hard miracle.

In those precarious days, they would see me receiving Don's gentleness and me relying on him. See their dad—who had ended the family we once all adored—sleep on the couch near the Christmas tree. See him gingerly walk up the stairs every hour or so to listen at the door to find out if I was up in my bed whimpering. See him wash every dish, wrap every present, fold every piece of laundry, empty every trash can. He would create a safe and beautiful harbor inside the most horrible storm.

As I agonized over this decision, I realized that my invitation was a signal to Connor and Lucy that this harbor their dad would shape—while flawed and full of heartbreak—was also kind and good. It was right. If I was going to exit their stories far too soon, my highest parenting priority was to create the most graceful and elegant bridge to their new normal, all four of us holding hands, even if it meant I would have to let go once we reached the other side. I would see them over to their new country and remind them how gorgeous and kind their country—their dad, their home—was and is, a beautiful man who wanted to do everything he could to help me physically heal.

I understood the logistics, but the stirring inside me indicated I was verging on a more profound reckoning, one in previous years I had managed to cleverly dance around, a coping mechanism to set aside the essence of light called *right.*

As I'd moved on from the ending of my marriage, I understood that my season of recovery and rebuilding hinged on the good and often agonizing journey toward forgiveness. I knew this language well; I had grown up in a house where this virtue was a cornerstone of our norms. "Do I forgive Don?" I would say to a friend who wondered how I was doing a year after the divorce. "Yes, well, it's a process. But, of course, that's all part of the healing."

I exuded this generous confidence in my gracious conversations, but I knew nothing of what I was talking about.

Instead, my inner thoughts swarmed obsessively as I replayed and replayed and replayed innocuous moments, painful moments, slights, glories, and devastations within our marriage. I cast myself as the victim of the drama and Don as the broken antagonist, more weak than malevolent. This was the narrative that had allowed me to breathe again: Don as a broken figure. And I was simply collateral damage of the awful choices set in motion by his failings. *Sure, I've forgiven Don*, I'd tell myself. *I've forgiven him for his weakness.*

That's not forgiveness.

Paul's lamp of *whatever is right* guided me to an exploration of truly setting *right* in motion.

Forgiveness is far more mysterious and magical. Forgiveness is seeing the person who has wronged you and then choosing to embrace the person as if they are entirely separate from what they wrought. It is saying, and believing, this: "I see you for all that you are. You are a child of God. Which is to say, a remarkable miracle. I no longer see your past actions; instead, I see only you. And now my gift to you is to enable you to begin your own reckoning for what led to these decisions, an open gateway for a season of coming to terms. There is no penance or judgment here. You will not have me correcting, admonishing, or litigating your reckoning. Instead, I simply see and hold your true self."

I agonized through this because I thought this forgiveness—this true forgiveness—would mean that I would disappear. Don would emerge whole and free—maybe even a hero of the story: *Look at how he cared for her when she was sick!*—when I wouldn't be able to shake the terrible damage done by his choice to live hundreds of miles away from us when I was healthy. If the narrative I held of having compassion for his weaknesses tumbled away, I feared I would as well.

I was wrong. This invitation to true forgiveness was not a diminishment; it was, instead, a place of peaceful strength.

I came to understand that this was the heart of what Paul meant by *right.* Forgiveness—in all of its unique circumstances and timelines—is the core of what it means to be set *right.* Rich forgiveness intentionally sets in motion a reckoning, a renewal. What's made new through forgiveness can very well shine the kind of light that makes it possible to see all the other virtues on Paul's list fully flourish, enabling the plot to turn. The writer Lewis Smedes said this on forgiveness: "Forgiving seems almost unnatural. Our sense of fairness tells us people should pay for the wrong they do. But forgiving is love's power to break nature's rule."

Throughout this grappling, I was more mindful of my own flaws and mistakes during our married years. As I came to embrace a new way of seeing Don—and my own failings—I grew nearer to a freedom that had eluded me since that cold January morning in 2013.

I came to see that betrayal took away a part of my past that I treasured, and cancer threatened to take away my future. But forgiveness might reveal an uncharted path. One made just for us.

I came to see that receiving Don's care might set in motion the opening of new chapters for Lucy and Connor to develop alongside their dad. This could be a legacy gift, one that might change generations. Even so, this was a gift wrapped in whispers rather than bright ribbons, quiet and deep acts of grace that would gently nudge their imaginations to create a restored family, one in which their own children might come to adore their Grandpa Don and all of his generous joy.

Right, then, in this last room, became a direction, a forward aim, and ultimately a transformational release. *Right* says this:

> *Find liberation in the truth that whatever story you inhabit, there will be more chapters. And those chapters will bring more joy than sorrow if you trust the mysteries of grace. This will take time. It may take a lot of time. There will be days of forward motion followed by days when the crushing memories will feel like a paralysis, a trap of stagnation.*

I grew to see this forward motion toward forgiveness more like how a sailboat tacks: a back-and-forth rhythm that, remarkably, results in progress toward the destination.

* * *

In the weeks before surgery, Jacquelline and I went for a walk. I unpacked it all with 500 percent more nuance than was required to convey the essential point. She—like always—listened well.

"Okay," she said. "It's clear Don needs to be your caregiver. You've thought this through. It's the right decision. You're moving into this deeper place of mercy and forgiveness, and it's extraordinary. But it still stings. I get it. So now this is about how you're going to move through it. I have one small, pragmatic tip for the moments when it may feel simply too hard."

"I'm ready."

"No, you're not. Because if you were ready, you wouldn't have spent the last forty-five minutes explaining a few basic realities to me. In those awful days when you're home from the hospital and in pain and utterly dependent on Don and your heart inevitably stumbles from forgiveness to resentment, I might suggest a time-honored technique to bridge you back. Be a guy. Compartmentalize the hell out of this mess. When Don is in your bedroom helping you change into clean clothes? Understand that he's doing a job. When you hear everyone laughing downstairs and it sounds like your old life and it's just awful because you're not a part of it? Turn on Netflix and pivot to something else. Do what a million guys in our life do all the time. Do what you need to do to accomplish the task at hand, and find a way to mentally focus yourself on other things while the hard thing is happening. Also, maybe give Don some lousy jobs. When's the last time anyone has hosed down the garbage cans? I bet Connor's closet could use reorganizing. These could be fascinating priorities for you to explore."

While I was coming to see Don for who he was—a miracle of a man who made some awful choices—Jacquelline understood that embracing Don again as a soul who, like all souls, had intrinsic goodness would be anything but a linear path. Compassion and space and a little compartmentalization now and again would become essentials.

She knew the most meaningful paths are seldom straight ones. The paths that teach, that push, that inspire, that make new are more like switchbacks. Jacquelline reminded me that with each step, with each bend, we ascend.

She was right. As always.

Whatever Is Pure

While my recovery was arduous and painful, my abdominal surgery was deemed a success. I emerged with a full lobe of my liver removed (I'll never not be amazed that the liver regenerates, and today it's the same size and just as healthy as it was way back before my diagnosis) and a slightly snipped colon. Or, as I liked to think of it: a semicolon. Clever and highly functional. Even a little bit elegant if used just right.

The pathology report from surgery was as encouraging as we could have wished for. All the margins were clear, which meant that the disease was contained, at least in my abdomen. Sebastien explained it this way: "Think of it like a block of cheese. If you see a little mold on the corner, and you slice around the mold and remove it—you can still eat the cheese." I mumbled something about how I tend to always throw out cheese that has a speck of mold on it, and he reminded me that this was strange given that some cheeses are a form of mold.

My follow-up CT scan, however, revealed a wrinkle. I had one stray met in the right upper lobe of my lung, near the edge. It was about one centimeter, meaning it had not only managed to dodge Foxy's jets but had grown a smidge since chemo was paused two months earlier.

I was heartbroken. I had come so far, and now the playbook seemed in jeopardy.

About a month after surgery, Sebastien and I went for a stroll. After listening patiently to all my anxiety and confusion, he said gently, "Remember I mentioned last summer you'd have a little cleanup work to do? In some ways, you're right on track with the playbook. Plus, the met is placed in an ideal spot. You'll have what's called a VATS wedge resection. It's an easy surgery. A chip shot, really. Probably not more than one day in the hospital."

"Do you think I'll need to do this soon? Or maybe after the final rounds of chemo?"

Sebastien was always careful in these moments, these times when I would ask him his opinion about the path before Colocci and others had had a chance to weigh in.

"You'll review the scans with Colocci next week, yes?"

"Yeah, I'll see her on Monday."

"Good. I'm sure she'll make the right call."

Colocci agreed that the best course for dealing with this isolated metastasis—now a familiar word in my lexicon—was a follow-up surgery, especially in this chemo-free window. She referred me to a reputable thoracic surgeon at Stanford.

Whenever a new medical character entered my stage, I approached them with all kinds of positivity. From the first hours of my diagnosis, I learned to respect every member of my team. I googled my new surgeon and discovered that he was the type to go for the full bio. Every degree, every honor, every paper ever published was there in a kind of infinity scroll of achievements. From that night on, he became Dr. Phenomenal. I arrived with giddy confidence to my first appointment, carrying a mix of respect and focus. I had a solid six months of surgery small talk with Sebastien in my hip pocket and could toss around phrases like *VATS wedge* and *chip shot* like the best of them.

He arrived in my exam room with one resident in tow.

"Hi, I'm Dr. Phenomenal. How are you feeling today?"

"Oh, hi! Yes, well—whew, it's been a lot—but, you know, bodies love to heal, and I'm now cruising around and feeling—well, I just might be the healthiest stage IV cancer patient—"

"Yes, okay," he cut me off. "I see that your cancer has metastasized to your lung, which is deeply problematic."

"But, um, wouldn't you agree it's positioned in an ideal place for a VATS wedge?"

He looked up from the scans to meet my eyes, perhaps a little impressed with my thoracic lingo.

"Yes, the VATS wedge is likely the path here. It's relatively straightforward, assuming we don't see any additional activity on your next scan."

"My next scan? But I just had a scan a few weeks ago."

"Yes, well, I need one more before operating. I need to make sure there's only this one met." He looked at his notes again, and then at me. "Do you have children?"

"Yes," I said. "Two teenagers. They are marvelous."

"I see." He paused and lowered his voice. "I'm sorry. It's a very difficult diagnosis. We'll do what we can."

I left rattled and unnerved and called Sebastien to see if there was something hiding in my scan that only Dr. Phenomenal could see that maybe the rest of us had missed.

"I know Dr. Phenomenal," Sebastien said. "He can be a little formal."

"So, maybe this is a normal Monday for him?"

"Maybe he had a tough case before you. Have you ever had an off Monday?"

"I've had plenty of off Mondays."

"Well, there you go. Listen, I have to run. You can find me later if you have more questions."

I stood in the lobby of the medical building, just steps from the hospital, a little frozen. I was exhausted by all of this, especially how desperately hard I was trying to get every medical person in my story to adore me. Like millions of other patients, I had convinced myself that if I formed some kind of kinship tie—or even the simplest of emotional bonds—my physician might care ever so slightly more, might summon the very heights of their A game for my case. Over time, I came to appreciate the perfectly healthy tension in play with this mindset—medicine requires immense trust between the patient and the physician, and yet this person examining me was called to this profession to care for me, regardless of whether we were emotionally bonded, regardless of whether I was charming. And yet kinship does matter as a part of the human experience. Another duality I learned to hold rather than resolve.

I had the scan performed and braced myself for the weight of the wait.

A pause here to sidebar about how scan results are now delivered to patients in our digital age of cost-cutting medical efficiency. Results are simply loaded into our patient portal and arrive in our life story via a push notification on our phone. I've gotten life-or-death news while waiting in line for a latte or navigating Trader Joe's, hours or sometimes days ahead of hearing from any medical professional calling to contextualize the news.

But for this CT scan, I eagerly waited all day Monday for the ping to deliver the narrative readout from the radiologist. By Tuesday afternoon, I put in a call to Dr. Phenomenal's office, and they assured me I would be receiving the results soon. My procedure was slated for Thursday, and I still hadn't been notified of when I was supposed to arrive.

Wednesday morning I called again. "I had a CT scan on Monday. Can you please release the data so I can review the findings?"

"Okay. I see here that Dr. Phenomenal has put a hold on releasing the results. I'm sorry I can't post them."

"What? But it's my data."

"I'm sorry. Dr. Phenomenal will call you later with more."

"No," I said, respectfully. "He can call me if he'd like, but I'm requesting that my data be released. Now."

The nurse sighed. She knew I could escalate this request, and all of this could get more complicated than it needed to be. "I hear you. I'll relay this request."

Within an hour, the push alert came to my phone. The narrative indicated a small group of new mets, none more than four millimeters. But their presence was ominous: the outlier now had friends, who would invariably grow.

Three hours later, my phone lit up with a call from Stanford University Medical Center. "Ms. Low? This is Dr. Phenomenal."

"Yes, hi. I've read through the report. Thanks for calling."

"Right, well, I would have preferred to walk you through this before you read the report," he said in a displeasured tone. "Unfortunately, you have more activity in your lung, so I won't be able to operate. There's no sense in removing one met when others are now present. The best medical advice I can tell you is to head back to chemo and hopefully that will keep the disease contained."

"Right, but the other mets are so small," I countered.

"That doesn't matter. They're there."

I stared out the window to my backyard garden, seeing traces of invasive wild mixed in with the hydrangeas and azaleas in full bloom. The occasional invader gave the flora—a bounty planted by a skilled gardener with an imaginative eye for color and texture—a sweeter meaning. The shrubs and flowers there by design flourished alongside the errors. Their colors had more to give because of the small threats toiling in their shared soil beds.

"Ms. Low? Are you still there?"

"Yes, I'm here."

"So, you understand your surgery is canceled for Thursday." Pause. "I wish you the best."

"Right. Okay. I appreciate your time." I hung up and walked outside to gaze in wonder at the deep pink of my winter azalea blossoms and spotted a stray weed. I spotted another invader, and then saw another. How many more winters would I have?

From hour one of my diagnosis, I had made sense of my disease by painting pictures in my mind, visual metaphors to help me see the larger story and understand the inevitable character shifts, plot details, whimsy, and absurdity. These metaphors not only gave me a way of seeing but also created narrative ribbons, like bandages, that could attend to my ever-growing wounds, even if only temporarily. My metaphorical narratives helped me to see the grander story; I could be in service to the plot. Maybe I could even help shape it or at least see it for what it was becoming.

Mostly, the gravity of my diagnosis required a proper intellectual home so I could make sense of "whys" that lived under the surface of the facts—facts that now arrived with each new scan. The metaphors in my mind became vessels that could hold the constant ambiguity and underlying fear; chaos could find a narrative purpose, which created space for me to rest while I slowly inched toward wisdom.

My marriage was once a messy and at times glorious garden. And so now were my lungs. Within the garden of my lungs, among the air sacs gorgeously called alveoli, the tiniest weeds were sprouting. At the time, none of us knew if these invading weeds were on a scorched-earth march or perhaps just tentatively sowing problematic seeds.

All we knew was that the scan showed multiple weeds growing within my miraculous forest of bronchial trees. And Dr. Phenomenal was a smart enough surgeon to know it would be a fool's errand to gaze out on a garden, see one problematic weed alongside a few smaller invaders, but pull only the one he could grasp. Why waste his highly accoladed skills to remove one sprig of wild when the garden had others on the move?

A devastation wave typically began in my arms and crested in my shoulders. By then I knew it was too late, the wave would pummel my chest only for my neck to collapse while my head dropped into my hands. The sobs were like carrying weights without end. All that effort, no forward motion.

And I was alone. Connor and Lucy were spending their winter break with Don in Orange County, an ideal plan for what we assumed would be a relatively easy follow-up surgery.

I texted Sebastien:

> Hi. Tough news here. Dr. Phenomenal is choosing not to operate. He saw some new mets. Can we connect at some point?

Three dots blinked.

Sebastien: What? He's pulling the case?

Me: Yup.

Sebastien: I'm in Houston and finishing a work dinner. I'll call you in a minute.

It was just a few seconds when the phone rang. "Hi. Okay, first—tell me where you are. Are you home?" I always thought this was a curious trait of Sebastien—he liked to know my location. My guess is that this question helped ground him. A place to begin. Any surgeon has to begin with the essential facts of the matter, and my physical whereabouts were as strong as any other toehold into the situation at hand.

"Yes, I'm at home."

"Are Connor and Lucy with you?"

"No. They're with their dad in Costa Mesa."

"So, you're alone?"

God, I hated that question. At once ordinary and yet laced with a searing indictment of vulnerability. "Yeah. I just got off the phone with Dr. Phenomenal."

"Tell me what he said."

"Well, it wasn't much. He just said he saw a few more mets, so it made no sense to operate. I mean that's it. I just need to start chemo again, which feels like delaying the inevitable. The thing we don't say out loud, but that we all know. I have a terrible disease and there's no cure and this whole project is mainly about putting a few more months on my doomed timeline."

"How many more mets?"

"What? I don't know. Hold on, I'm reading the radiologist's report—I guess five or so. They're all small."

Sebastien was quiet as I updated him and then rushed into speculating about my odds of making it to Connor's high school graduation.

"Okay, so I'm looking at flights. I'm trying to see if I can catch a late flight tonight but the last one is at nine and it's already eight here, so I don't think I can make it."

I started to cry again, but this time my tears were quiet and full of relief. Sebastien and I were engaged in a new dance. Our friendship had been growing closer as I was inching ever nearer to release from cancer jail, but we dutifully played our parts onstage, never breaking the fourth wall to explore where this friendship might be headed.

"Oh, you're lovely, but I wouldn't want you to interrupt your trip to come back because of this."

"It's no trouble. My meetings tomorrow here aren't all that important. Tell you what, I can get on an early flight, so I could get back to San Francisco by about ten in the morning. Do you want to connect tomorrow and talk this through?"

"If it's truly no trouble. This would mean the world. Yes, I could pick you up at the airport."

"Sure, if you want. I mean, we can decide tomorrow. I can easily Uber and just meet you someplace."

A classic Sebastien move. He'd open up a new trail on our unconventional friendship map only to pause and suggest maybe the familiar and safer map was the more reliable one.

I picked him up at the airport and asked him to drive. After some back-and-forth about where we were headed, we settled on a walk through Golden Gate Park, which meant going to Sebastien's house first to drop things and change shoes. We found our way into his kitchen, where I shared the narrative report.

"So, it's a setback," he conceded. "But I think it's key not to be too alarmed here. This is common and there are all kinds of reasons to think chemo will work again, and if you need surgery in your lung, that will still be an option."

As we moved from his kitchen down the steep hills of his neighborhood and into the local greenways, he indulged my interrogations, a series of not more than three questions that I managed to ask in dozens of different ways. His patience was as unending as the water moving through the park's main fountain—reliable, with just enough new nuance in each drop—and I eventually found my way to quiet.

A couple of hours later, we found a bench to sit with it all. He opened his arms so I could find a space for my head on his shoulder, my own mini rock of Gibraltar. After a few moments, Sebastien offered something new. "I think it's time for you to know Andrew Ko," he said.

"Andrew who?"

"Ko. Dr. Ko. He's an extraordinary oncologist based at UCSF. His focus is abdominal cancers, and I believe he has precise knowledge of how these cancers behave in the lung. He could be a smart person to add to your team."

"Okay, sure. Why not?" I sat up straighter. "Actually, I wonder what Colocci would think about me bringing on someone new. Be honest here. What *do* doctors think when patients go chasing after second opinions?"

Sebastien answered first in all the appropriate and safe ways. "The most important thing is the patient. So, if they think a second opinion is warranted, then it is."

"Uh-huh. But *really*. I mean, do you guys kind of roll your eyes when patients do this, or are you secretly relieved?"

He wouldn't really bite, but he offered a few clues. "Look. This isn't like buying a car or something, when a sales agent would be pissed to know you love the new model of an Acura only to find out that you just left to go look at a BMW. It's more like—more information is usually good to have. And if another physician has more to offer, then have at it. Honestly, sometimes it's a relief. Usually the second opinion mirrors yours, so it's a nice way to get confirmation."

With that, we labored up the impossibly steep hills back to his house. In his kitchen, Sebastien opened his laptop, which had a day's worth of emails that needed attention. I had a phone full of calls and texts wondering how my nonexistent surgery had gone.

It was time for me to drive home. Sebastien had given me his day, his wisdom, his companionship. What he didn't offer was closer intimacy, even though we continued to straddle the line. I was still in cancer jail, and we both knew it.

He walked me out to my car, holding my hand as I carefully stepped down what felt like a ninety-degree angle on his street. He pulled me close for a long and final hug.

"Thank you for this," I said. "For coming back and helping me sort this all out."

"You bet. No problem."

He leaned down, gave me a familiar kiss, and said to text him when I got home.

Clicking through Andrew Ko's biography proved to be another cartwheel through the grassy lawn of oncological overachievers. Impressive academic pedigree, awards, publications, a summary of research interests that read like Dr. Ko just might save us all.

As captivated as I was by Dr. Ko on paper, though, I was far more enchanted by him in person. He heard me out on the entire saga before saying, "What I see here in your lungs are small mets—ditzels, really—and for now it seems like the overall disease burden is quite low. I think that's reassuring."

I listened carefully, letting my mind wander briefly to the charming lexical quirk of how we name things that are small. Visser called them "schmaltzies." Ko called them "ditzels."

I preferred "itty-bitties" and sometimes "teeny-tinies." Sebastien liked to say "those little guys."

I refocused as Ko underscored that Dr. Phenomenal's recommendation to move back to a few rounds of chemo was the right approach, but he previewed a possible new path. "I think it makes sense to take on three or so more rounds of chemotherapy—that's important to do regardless," he said, echoing Visser's original playbook instructions. "And after that you'll be ready for another scan. If that outlier met is still there, I see no reason why we wouldn't revisit a conversation about surgery, and you could do that here at UCSF."

Driving back from San Francisco to Menlo Park, I had forty-five minutes to replay the layers of subtext in my back-and-forth with Ko. He told me—essentially—the same thing as Dr. Phenomenal, but I left my time with him soaring with hope, whereas my experience with Dr. Phenomenal was a case study in sorrow. But why?

Too often in medical stories, we slot our physicians into unhelpful archetypes. Are you for me or annoyed by me? Are you my champion or the one who all of my friends will say "Yuck. *So glad* you got that second opinion!" about?

We do this to level the playing field I suspect. Physicians live in a different realm. They hold information and a degree of wisdom the rest of us lack, plus an unbalanced responsibility for our lives. If we can pronounce one doctor *the savior of the story* and another *the rude one who just couldn't do the job*, we can fool ourselves into feeling a sense of control.

The reality is that most physicians are marvelous. They've worked harder than most of us who chose other careers, plus something stirred in their hearts at a young age that drew them close to the virtue of healing.

I completed a few more courses of chemo. As Ko predicted, the minusculements diminished, so we arranged to have my small lung surgery performed at UCSF.

The surgery date coincided with the annual Met Gala in New York City, so I decided I was having a met gala of my own at UCSF. Fewer ballgowns, but perhaps more smiles when I heard the procedure went as planned, and the met was easily excised with no other suspicious activity to be seen nearby.

After a grueling forty-eight hours in the hospital, I was exhausted, sore, and desperately wanting to go home. There was a little back-and-forth about a lingering air pocket near the surgery site that needed some attention, but finally, a deal was struck. Sebastien helped greenlight my discharge, but under the condition I stay at his house that night. If anything went awry, he would be there, and we were just ten minutes from UCSF. Deal.

I slowly entered his home feeling like a wounded and badly bruised warrior stumbling back from the front lines. After a delicious sojourn napping on his couch in front of his fireplace, I eventually found the strength to stand and navigate the stairs with Sebastien's help. I collapsed into the basement bed.

The next morning marked a fleeting milestone: for at least that day, I had no detectable cancer.

* * *

The weeks that followed brought long summer days and a new paradox to add to my list: as I tasted a renewed (albeit fragile) sense of health, the rest of the world around me was spiraling. On the coasts, COVID caseloads were surging, and the messaging from the White House was a mix of chaotic and reckless.

While I was experiencing the sheer awe and glory of medicine, it felt as if the raucous public square had become poisoned by influential amateurs, characters who preferred to cast doubt on science and data. That summer I read posts and tweets by COVID skeptics and wondered: *Have any of these people ever had a troublesome scan? Would any of these science deniers say no to anesthesia before a lifesaving surgery? Or have their doctors unmask during that surgery?* I knew the poison the skeptics had unleashed would lead to an untold number of unnecessary deaths, which felt insane to me as I fought so hard to stave off my own.

Within all the uncertainty, though, I also found silent kinship with the hundreds of thousands testing positive for COVID and the millions navigating the crushing uncertainty. All those anxious glances masked people gave each other standing in grocery lines? I knew those looks, intimately. That look was mine every time I greeted a nurse who sauntered in to take my vitals or any time a new test result was pushed to my phone.

The world around me confronted questions that were all too familiar to me: What happens if I get sick? Who looks after my loved ones? Who's the best doctor to call? Which expert has the best data sets, the sharpest insight?

Naturally, I wondered if I was more vulnerable to contracting COVID but was assured that I was basically in a normal risk group. My medical team told me to be safe, but not run for a bunker; my labs were close to precancer healthy baselines. So, while nearly everyone else made their worlds smaller and became more cautious, for the first time in ten months, I woke up feeling well and dazzled by the notion that I was—at least temporarily—healthy. I wanted to live as fully, and as expansively, as possible.

What's more, as global anxiety about personal health skyrocketed to historic levels, my own anxiety level eased.

Welcome to my planet! I would think.

Also: *It's terrible, but there are paths here to joy. Pull on those yoga pants and don't for a second worry that you haven't worn pants with a zipper in more than a month. It's entirely okay.*

And: *Know that the healers among us are war horses. While you Zoomed with colleagues this morning, nurses and lab techs and ER doctors were climbing into their cars for a grueling shift, some even dying to extend our days. Even now, scientists are working with barely a pause to fast-track a vaccine that will save billions of lives in service to one noble miracle: a breakthrough to extend these fragile, excruciating, forever hopeful days. They're bringing their brilliance to create more days. They are doing this for you.*

Mainly this: *This fear you are feeling? It may not go away for a long time. But there's a gentle message revealed in that trepidation—it's the best reminder of all that you have precious gifts in your life you don't want to lose. Take care of those gifts, like never before. Remember how delicious it feels to savor them.*

Connor and Lucy were seventeen and fifteen, and like nearly all teenagers on Planet Pandemic, they spent the summer at home, creating innovative and redemptive hacks to live their best lives within the lockdowns. Connor formed a new jazz band and convinced a local restaurant they'd be an ideal choice for outdoor Sunday brunch; within two weeks, all outside tables were booked and Menlo Park had live music to look forward to each weekend. Lucy found a way to have dance classes over Zoom in our small living room, high kicks in-between couches and a coffee table.

Sebastien and I formed our own COVID pod during lockdown—long walks and longer dinners were our routine. Our relationship defied all my familiar conventions—he had begun as a romantic interest who swiftly pivoted to a medical friend, expert, and advocate. And then a new path emerged. As we bounced through medical mileposts—chemo rounds, surgery, scans, surprises, setbacks, steps forward, surgery again—we had formed an uncanny friendship. We could discuss the most intimate of my medical mysteries, and I could ask all the hardest questions, and yet most of our conversations were about our shared passions: careers devoted to bettering lives at scale, raising nearly adult children, art, politics, having eyes to spot miracles practically begging to be discovered.

We set up our camp on the edge of intimacy. Unconventional realities—a pandemic and cancer—created both a safe haven and a barrier as we drew ever closer.

Throughout our hikes and meals, we explored all the big ideas and our vastly different vantage points.

Sebastien was Black, had attended elite private schools on the East Coast, and had gone on to soar academically through the Ivy League. If there was a medical school path paved with excellence, he found it and conquered it. He spent part of his residency years in Paris, where his French was perfect enough to direct the nuance of fast orders in an operating room.

I was a girl raised in the suburbs of San Diego. My public schools were a mixed bag of serviceable to terrific. Our family budget was always tight, so a family vacation meant hours in a station wagon on our way to some kind of Christian camp, which usually proved to be more about joy and grace than some narrow aperture of right and wrong. I chose a liberal arts Christian college that provided academic rigor despite its lack of prestige or name recognition; it felt like coming home the minute I stepped on its campus in Montecito, California.

In those wrenching weeks of summer in 2020, when our nation moved through a season of racial reckonings following the murder of George Floyd, Sebastien and I naturally marveled at our different kaleidoscopes for how we were both seeing, and living, those days.

He grew up with academic privilege. I grew up trotting through uneven public school terrain. He grew up with divorce. I grew up with parents who were happily married and a dad who constantly cheered on my good progress, who taught me about the power of persistent hope—and how to keep score—through the magic of baseball, with years of sitting in the cheap seats watching the Padres. Sebastien fast-tracked to professional acclaim from his earliest days. I spent my twenties patiently gaining wisdom while I found my calling. I walked through any hotel lobby wearing my workout clothes en route to the gym without a second's thought. He sometimes crossed the lobby dressed for the gym with intentional accessories—a towel, a water bottle—to make it clear to hotel strangers where he was headed. The counter vantage points made for substantive sparring matches when we dove into topics around language and inclusivity, power and politics.

We found an easy comfort in pointing out each other's quirks. If Sebastien could find a fancy phrase to replace a common notion, he would eagerly make it his own. An organization was never "low on cash"; rather, it was "dealing with an extended period of resource constraints." I found this adorably odd.

He was just as adept at pointing out my absurdities. On a hike, I opined about a daily miracle unfolding in front of us all and wondered why he wasn't equally as captivated by it. "Sebastien, think of this. Every day all nine billion of us have access to Wordle, and can you believe we love each other so much that no one dares spoil it by shouting out the word from the Twitter rooftops first thing in the morning?"

"Okay. First, realize you're off by a solid billion people on the planet. And I won't even go into percentages around English speakers and people with smartphones and the even smaller slice of people who find the game interesting. I guess you're off by about 8.95 billion, but sure, you make a thoughtful point about humanity's shared sense of connectivity when it comes to word games."

Our conversations elegantly and reliably pole-vaulted from the trivial to the transcendent. Few topics remained out of reach. Sitting on his fireside couch, on a San Francisco hilltop, next to a bay window that revealed the faithful arches of the Golden Gate Bridge in the distance, we'd settle into hours exploring new conversational territory. When we'd speak of medicine and mystery, wonder rolled in like the San Francisco fog—comforting and unsettling in equal measure. I was in awe of medicine, a discipline I was just discovering. I could ask Sebastien anything and he'd have a revelatory reply.

"Can you get knee cancer?" I'd ask.

"Yes, all the time," he'd say.

"My whole life I've never heard of anyone getting knee cancer. I think you ought to ask the Google about this."

"Diffuse and localized synovial sarcoma tumors can happen," he would reply.

"Have you ever witnessed a miracle in the OR?" I once asked.

"Miracles are ever present, but they usually have a complex and rational backstory. So, sure. You can call all kinds of things miracles, and I suppose I've heard others describe OR moments within that vein."

"No—I mean a true miracle. One that can't be explained," I responded.

"Most medical moments can be explained," he said.

"I think Visser is a miracle. I think his care and expertise all have a logical backstory, one grounded in devotion and hard work. But still, he's a miracle. As are his tailored suits."

"Okay, sure. I suppose it's just your use of the word. You're welcome to call anything a miracle."

"My friend Tracy. She and I were pregnant at the same time with our daughters. When we were five months pregnant, I was in Italy with Don for a vacation and stopped into an internet café to check my email. I saw a note from Tracy with terrible news. Her sonogram had revealed a diaphragmatic hernia, there was a gap, and the baby's intestinal organs were growing without the diaphragm to keep them in place, and they were encroaching on her lungs. Tracy's medical team strongly advised her to have an abortion. The baby—if she survived in utero—likely wouldn't live more than a few hours."

Sebastien listened patiently, nodding.

"So, there I was, in Florence, reading this email and I was devasted. Our babies were the same weeks along, and while I could feel my baby kicking, Tracy was five thousand miles away in absolute agony."

"I'm so sorry. Those are rare and always tragic pregnancy complications."

"Well, actually," I said. "She chose to continue the pregnancy and care for her unborn daughter. She was surrounded in prayer. Thousands of us prayed. And Baby Anna was born, alive. And get this—she survived more than a few hours. And then even a few days. Incredibly, the pediatricians determined that the diaphragm muscle had nearly closed—not all the way, but almost. The baby was in critical condition when she was born, and she needed a corrective surgery. For months, she had to be on a feeding tube.

But she survived, and then she thrived. Today Anna is sixteen and she's a delight. This is a miracle, wouldn't you agree?"

Sebastien was quiet. "There are many mysteries in the body. I'm so glad there was a positive outcome in this case."

"But you wouldn't call it a miracle?"

"I think you can call it all sorts of things," he said.

"Okay, yes. But I wonder if we could take a step back here. How about stories of miracles within the gospels?" I asked. "Take Lazarus. Maybe the most famous miracle Jesus performed. He brought Lazarus back to life, four days after he had died. We have a historic record of this—it's the miracle that put Holy Week in motion."

Sebastien had grown up in the Catholic Church and was well aware of the story of Lazarus, so he didn't need me to fill in additional nuance or historical proofs. "Yes, I know the story. But there's an easy explanation here. Lazarus wasn't actually dead."

"What? Hold up. The entire story is about him being dead. Super dead. Mourners were gathered. His sisters were in agony. I mean, how hard is it to tell if someone is dead or not?"

"In the ancient world alive people were confused for being dead all the time," Sebastien said. "That was incredibly common. It's actually more complicated to tell if someone is dead than you might think."

My head was spinning. Sebastien had an uncanny ability to pivot a focused conversation—can medical miracles happen or not—to a twisty third angle, one that was just jarring and captivating enough that it could settle our differing vantage points with a convenient, and often fascinating, new tangent. This was a clever and often useful method to keep our discussions tethered to the next topic rather than careening into a ditch of quiet. But it was also a dodge. A way of having it both ways. I imagined he polished this conversational skill as he trained to become a surgeon. He learned how to acknowledge a question, answer it fairly, and then gently move the discussion to a subtle new vantage point. Or sometimes to a graceful conclusion.

Sebastien could carefully nudge our marathon-session discussions to safe places to avoid an impasse. I could tuck a question about my latest scan in small talk about one of my kids. We both knew what the other was up to with all those dialogue pivots. We indulged them.

Over time, though, our discussions were more often like a dazzling dance—charming, surprising, and full of spins. We were close, we were finishing each other's sentences, we were in sync. But just as audiences wonder whether the gold medalists are a couple off the floor, it was equally impossible to tell with us. All any of us could know for certain was the pirouette.

Like everyone else, by late July 2020 we grew restless and stir-crazy. I decided to book the kids and me a string of days in Tahoe for much-needed mountain air. What better place to follow the friendly advice COVID kept telling us—slow down and spend more time outside? We hiked, kayaked, attempted an impossible thousand-piece puzzle, and had a generally wonderful time.

What I didn't tell them, though, was that Sebastien and I had been texting about him joining me for the last three days after the kids would meet up with Don. Our texts were as casual and ambiguous as our times together.

Me: You're welcome to join me for a long weekend in the Sierras. Weather is perfect!

Sebastien: I'd love to—if it's not too much trouble?

Me: No trouble at all. I have a two-bedroom condo. We can hike or not hike, talk or not talk, cook or not cook. It's summer and a pandemic. Who doesn't want to be in Tahoe?

Sebastien: Exactly.

So, Sebastien was coming to Tahoe. Our intimate couch times that we never spoke of—would they pour over to Tahoe or would this simply be a time for two dear friends to breathe in mountain air and maybe assemble an impossible puzzle?

I had no idea and even-keeled expectations. My health was still so uncertain—I had a scan coming up in just ten days—that I made every effort not to grow attached to any future and its fictional stories. All I cared about was squeezing out every morsel of the day.

He arrived late Thursday night, fresh off the three-hour drive from San Francisco. We had never actually spoken of his arrival in any detail; we avoided details, because details would open doorways to *What are we doing?* Exploring that question might stop the dance, and we had no appetite for that.

We had plans for an afternoon hike down to Emerald Bay. We descended a precarious and winding trail; eventually, our hiking boots hit the lakeshore sand, and we settled onto a log to gaze at a sapphire-blue bay that someone, sometime, declared Emerald.

Sitting next to him, glancing up at his profile, I realized Sebastien embodied that *Talking Heads* lyric—he had a face with a view. Everything about him embodied hope. He had a strong track record in the lifesaving department, and our companionship opened up a new place in my heart, the best reminder that there was more life to be discovered.

Underneath, I was self-aware enough to know that I was playing my own mental game: I viewed the more time Sebastien spent with me, the closer we were becoming, as perhaps a clue about his overall confidence about my future. We sat on our Emerald Bay log musing about the yachts and how Rule Number One of the pandemic was to not post pics on a yacht while the rest of your friends were stuck at home on their couches. We didn't talk about cancer. But as I stared out into the blue, I remembered how I often told my closest friends that navigating cancer felt like climbing a mountain. Hard but possible. Incremental steps and steep inclines. Occasional meadows. I made a mental note: *Those views from the mountain you promised to notice? This is one of them. Don't miss it.*

We cooked that night and managed to get two corners worked out on the World's Most Impossible Puzzle. A longer kiss, a longer linger, longer ambiguity. Still, a parting. We were playing a new dynamic of our game. Naming it would end it, I was certain of that. And I wasn't interested in endings.

Saturday was as perfect as an August day in Tahoe can deliver, so we made a plan to rent a Jet Ski. We had spent enough time gazing at the lake; now it was time to get on it. As we signed our lives aways on multiple pages of waivers, Sebastien said, in passing, that this was going to be his first time on a Jet Ski. We had opted for a double, so I reminded him I was terrific at putting my life in someone else's hands.

We started out tentatively, sorting out balance and speed and dodging kayakers close to the shore. But then Sebastien flicked both wrists back and we were a rocket on the lake. Speed skimming and me with my arms locked around his stomach for dear life. It was more like leaping than Jet Skiing. Or maybe the leaps were so grand it was closer to flying.

The blue sky held hands with the blue lake, and Sebastien and I were inside their clasp. Joy felt wrapped around me as tightly as I was wrapped around Sebastien, and nothing could have persuaded me to let go. On that lake, in that moment, I gave myself permission to simply say thank you.

That night, we repeated our ambiguous goodnight ritual, and I walked off to my room, exhausted and thrilled by the game. But within minutes of me turning off my light, Sebastien climbed into my bed, breaking through the ambiguity with a new world of expert tenderness and intimacy.

We were fully alive, fully in each other's arms.

And then. He pushed away, or rather, he somehow pushed me away. Or did he? What was happening? I looked over and Sebastien was on his back, breathing deeply. Silent.

"What is it?" I whispered while wiping away a tear he couldn't see.

Silence.

I was done. If the wall was to come down, now was the time. I sat up.

"Okay, Sebastien. One of three things is happening here. One, you're not attracted to me, and I don't think that's it. Two, you're with someone else, which wouldn't make much sense because, then, why aren't you with her? Or three, you know my cancer is lethal and you're not about to open up anything real with someone who's going to be exiting this world in a matter of months. So, which is it?"

"Let's talk about it tomorrow. I'm sorry." He left the bedroom.

After hours of churning, when the sun began to rise, I found some clothes, packed my bag, and sat outside on the little deck off of my bedroom. I put on headphones to listen to music, the same music I would listen to during chemo rounds. Sounds to escape dread and the misery that ran so deep I could feel its pulse. About a half hour later, I heard Sebastien in the kitchen and what sounded like him packing up. He came out to the balcony.

"Oh, hey there! You want some coffee? Have you been up long?"

"Yeah, I've been up a while."

"Great, okay. Hey, I'm just cleaning up the kitchen. Do you want to take the leftovers from last night or just dump them? That pasta was pretty good, so you might want to take it home with you."

I stared out at the mountains.

"Amy? Is there anything else I can pack up?"

"You're seriously chitchatting about leftovers, Sebastien? I gave you an easy multiple-choice question last night. I think I deserve an answer."

Sebastien sat down, sighed, and stared at his feet. "Okay. This is hard." He was quiet and then finally got on with it. "I am with someone else. I met her a few months after your diagnosis, before your surgery. She doesn't live in San Francisco, and I wasn't sure where it was all headed, but I'm with her now. Please know you're so dear to me, and I'm sorry if we crossed lines."

I was breathing, but I'm not sure how. And then the realization hit me that I had unwillingly become the other woman. I gasped for breath in panic, my mind racing to gauge my complicity. How bad was this? Was there any moral equivalency to what had happened in my marriage? My eyes managed to refocus. It was far too soon to explore any of those awful questions. There was only sorrow.

I stood, muttered something about the leftovers, and packed my remaining items. I was so tired. Tired of being sick, of dancing with Sebastien, of telling myself to be charming for Ko and Colocci, of making up for Don's decision not to co-parent near his children, of forever finding the bright side of chaotic and relentlessly returning darkness.

Sebastien caught up with me as I loaded my bags in the car. We sat near flower boxes outside before heading home in our separate cars.

"So. Is she lovely?" I asked him.

"Yes," he said.

"I believe she lives in a college town, right?"

"How did you know that?"

"About two months ago I was at your house and your phone rang. I glanced over and saw her name on your phone, a name you've never mentioned. I remember that day you stepped out to make a fast call, and I remembered feeling—for just two minutes—the way I used to feel with Don. But instead of asking you about it, I quietly googled her name and decided I didn't want to know any more. I decided that if she mattered, you'd of course tell me about her. You never did, and I chose not to ask. I did this knowing that me not asking was a form of complicity. I decided maybe it was okay not to care, because I knew nothing and because I live scan to scan—ninety days at a time—and everything about that skews your sense of moral clarity.

"So, if the person I googled is the person you're with, I know she lives in another state, she's quite accomplished, and the two of you probably have a few shared passions, and you are likely inside of a grand romance. It must be glorious. I imagine the two of you talk about your futures with all kinds of ease and familiarity."

Sebastien stayed quiet, staring just above my head.

"It's curious, isn't it, that you and I avoid small talk about the future. We've gotten good at that. Because we both know I—and we—don't have one."

"That's not the reason," he said. He was emphatic about how my diagnosis had no bearing, but we both knew the more he doubled down on this point, the more insincere it sounded.

About three months earlier, in the midst of one of our sublime couch-by-the-fire times—when we crossed into new physical terrain, but always with an abrupt pivot to a goodbye—I had voiced the unspoken: "You know, Sebastien, these sudden goodbyes are a rejection."

"Oh, this isn't rejection," he'd said back then. "We have abundant care and connection, and you're so very dear to me." And then, "I realize we can sometimes get a little ahead of ourselves here. But we have a delicate dynamic. I'm a doctor and I'm providing input on your case. I learned long ago I can't mix those domains within a romantic relationship."

I'd sat on the couch and stared into the fire and thought, *God, how pathetically lame and how intellectually insulting.* Sebastien wasn't my doctor, and he was playing a game where he was attempting to have it all ways—adoring friend, physical intimacy without clear meaning, heroic medical adviser. In my own hurt, I found his selfishness off-putting and cold. How many times did I end an evening at his house the same way: I would stand up, put on my shoes, smile, and say I appreciated all the help he had offered to my case over the past many months, leaving the residual awkwardness of an abrupt goodbye unsaid. Instead, I clung to incomplete intimacy because I knew my disease relegated me to a world of romantic isolation; I couldn't abandon our friendship because his medical guidance was unparalleled.

We chose not to conclude the conversation then. Instead, we gently paused it, knowing there were more days ahead to be lived, even within constant fragility.

But sitting out near the Tahoe wildflowers, I unpaused what we'd left dangling several months back.

"Sebastien, stop." He flinched. "Look, here we are among all of these colors, these firecracker flowers, all this life. We've had quite a time. But there's a wasp in our midst, and its sting is disproportionately aimed at me. It's not cancer. It's how we've set up a compartmentalized relationship. We've kept pieces of our truth off-limits, even while we've said yes to physical romance. To be clear, I've gone along with all of this, slowly settling for a dynamic that's inconsistent with who I am and lowering my own relational bar. This all comes with a dear price. And today, I'm the one who's paying it."

He looked away.

"So, here's the most important thing I can say here, with these mountain wildflowers and a wasp circling my heart. My days—however many I have left—are precarious. I've chosen to live these days with a grand and open heart. A hopeful heart. A heart so hopeful that I haven't even given up on the chance for love again, even with this awful diagnosis. There are a million reasons for this, but one overwhelms all the others. God almighty, this mountain. This mountain I'm climbing. It's so mighty, so full of mystery, and pain, and exhaustion. But it's revelatory. I'm seeing views that are too important and miraculous not to share. It's more than sharing, though. It's a desire to bring an intimate beloved close. To join. To whisper this, late at night: *Can I tell you what I'm seeing? Can you draw closer, ever closer? There is deep joy, and deep fear, in this space. Will you be brave and hold my hand within these most daunting spaces? Will you embrace the grandest equation of all—that fierce love is worth profound pain?*

"None of us really ever says this next thing out loud, but I get to say anything right now, so here goes. Romance is magnificent for all the millions of reasons we know. But it's most magical when you're climbing this overwhelming mountain of mine. If you're summoned to this mountain with a committed beloved, treasure this gift as mightily as you can. We say 'in sickness and in health' as if it's a trope of some kind. It's not. It's by far the most sacred of vows.

"So you should love her well. You should be with her completely. Someday you might get sick. When you do, you'll want her close. Having her close then means investing completely in her today. This means not dancing with me.

"And if we ever find our way to a true friendship, you should tell me all about her. You should tell me stories about how much you adore her because of her extraordinary intellect. And I'll be so very happy for you. That's how true friends would talk. And behave.

"I don't know if we'll ever be friends like that," I continued. "I don't know anything. Wait, that's not true. I do know something. I know I have a scan on Friday. I know that I'm going alone, and

I'll be alone when I meet with Visser and he walks me through what he sees."

"Would you like me to go with you?" he asked, relieved we were talking about a scan and not how clearly brokenhearted I was.

"No. I don't know. I don't really care, honestly. I'm just so tired, Sebastien. Tired of all of this."

I stood up.

"There were some beautiful moments in the past couple of days," I said. "Someday when I think of Tahoe, I'll think of us flying on that Jet Ski, and only that. For now, I can only think about how sad all of this is. It's time to go."

We each drove away from the Sierras and down to our respective homes in the Bay Area.

I had three terrible hours in my car to play these months with Sebastien over and over in my mind. In some ways, this was familiar territory. In the previous six years, I'd had a rich dating life. I'd met lovely men, grew attached, then detached when I knew the decision was right, and had others gracefully detach from me. That was dating. Full of hope and risk and heartbreak and hope all over again.

But this dynamic with Sebastien was unique.

Who on earth starts sort of dating a surgeon just weeks before receiving a devastating cancer diagnosis that ends up settling in her lungs—said surgeon's specialty—and said surgeon likes blurring lines and keeping options open and said patient keeps beating the odds and living and feeling fabulous and then said surgeon keeps saving her life so she's naturally drawn to all that he inhabits and then a pandemic descends and the world becomes slower and more intimate, which means dozens of hikes and long dinners and time on the couch by the fire? And then we find out he's actually dating someone exceptional who happens to live thousands of miles away. I mean, has this happened before? If so, how did it all work out?

Maybe it wasn't all that unique. Maybe this is why Paul tucked *pure* into his list of virtues for his beloved friends in Philippi. Did Paul know of a handsome doctor in Philippi who had struck up a blurry friendship with someone remarkable in that community but who had decided to keep it all conveniently compartmentalized? Did Paul know—centuries ago—that an intentionally asymmetrical friendship is the antithesis of pure? Did he know that sometimes compartmentalization in relationships can be helpful? And could he discern when it becomes harmful?

I worked with this word—*pure*—all those 228 miles home. Why did Paul give it such prominence? What last-room vantage point elevated it so high?

At its essence, *pure* tells us something is free of contaminants. It's reliable. "Pure drinking water" is clean, healthy, cleansing. *Pure* is also rare and, therefore, valuable.

All around Tahoe you'll see bumper stickers that say KEEP TAHOE BLUE, a slogan of sorts, and a rallying cry. The community there delights in seasonal tourists, but its opening salvo is a plea to keep their magnificent lake pure. The Keep Tahoe Blue community describes their work this way: "We protect and restore the environmental health, sustainability, and scenic beauty of the Lake Tahoe Basin. We focus on water quality and its clarity for the preservation of a pristine Lake for future generations."

Health. Scenic beauty. Quality. Clarity. A pristine lake.

But two words stand apart: *future generations*. The Tahoe community understands that their work might come with short-term costs—investments, really—that will pay dividends for residents who don't yet even call Tahoe home.

Pure, then, comes with a command: it must be fiercely protected today for a healthy and pristine tomorrow.

Friendships are inherently messy because we all bring our harvest of flaws and delights to each person we encounter. As I continued to drive south, I wondered whether aiming for purity in a friendship—no matter its form—was too high a bar. Maybe Sebastien and I were just untangling from a common season of getting tangled up, following millions of others who overstepped and undercommunicated.

I got home, unpacked, and climbed into bed. Connor and Lucy were still away and I was grateful to have a quiet home while my heart was heaving.

The diagnosis of this mess was obvious. Sebastien and I had intentionally blurred the lines between friendship and romance. We quietly gave ourselves permission to exist within discordance. We made an awful bargain: we compartmentalized in a destructive way, picking and choosing which doors we'd open and which would stay locked. We layered in romance, but we abandoned the transparency and trust that romance offers—a gateway to an exclusive new home, a place with an unlimited expanse of rooms to inhabit.

I understood that a gifted surgeon naturally needed to be skilled in compartmentalization. In the operating room, the right measure of emotional detachment saved lives. Did Sebastien's talent for compartmentalization spill into multiple dynamics of his life? Or just with me?

I would never know. All I knew then was that we had contaminated what could have been pure. It was my first inkling that here in my last room I was growing strangely comfortable with short-term and impulsive decisions—ones that came with hard costs.

I stared at the ceiling, shivering. Love comes with risk. An open heart is an alive heart.

Whatever Is Lovely

My friend Michael Murphy is a famous architect. He's designed monuments, memorials, libraries, critically acclaimed buildings. But his best work is hospitals in Rwanda and Haiti. More than 1.7 million people have viewed the TED Talk in which Michael proclaimed this truth: Buildings can hurt, and buildings can heal. A building that can heal is concerned with ventilation. A building that can harm is concerned with short-term additions ill-equipped to solve long-term needs. A building that can heal is centered on the patient. A building that can harm is more focused on the passersby.

I've spent time in Stanford's two hospitals—the one designed by Edward Durrell Stone and the new hospital designed by Rafael Viñoly Architects—and I received excellent medical care in both buildings. When I was diagnosed I spent several early days in the old hospital; I had my surgery in the new hospital, which had opened just days before. One hospital infused my heart with hope, while the other crushed my spirit.

I asked Michael to help me understand why my experiences in the two buildings were so radically different. He met me once to walk around and inside both buildings to wrestle with whether the structures themselves had anything to do with the business of hope.

We began in the new hospital. "Look, here," Michael said, pointing to a map of the layout. "Do you see how the building is configured as a cross layered on top of another cross? The configuration enables all the patient rooms to face outward. All the patient rooms have a window, have light. That's unusual."

We then moved back to the main atrium, which to me felt like walking into the primary entrance of the Louvre. The ceiling was made of glass, so light cascaded throughout. The light created warmth, clarity, a sense of soaring. The light enabled an environment for hope. We could see up, around, through, and within.

"Yes," I said. "After my surgery I was in a private room—all the rooms here are private, I believe—and the window looking out on the hills of Silicon Valley was massive. How many sunrises and sunsets did I enjoy? That view reminded me that I need to rejoin it all." Some mornings I'd imagined those sidewalk chalk paintings from *Mary Poppins*, and how I wanted to simply jump into the day that was coming to life outside my hospital window.

We then walked down a short greenway to Stanford's old hospital, Stone's design. Along the way Michael paused to examine the exterior—the sides of the building are covered with an elaborate concrete mosaic. Michael called it a screen, and he wanted a closer look.

"Do you see how the patterns in this concrete screen repeat? I bet the pattern mirrors the interior floor plan. This is very Stone," he said. "He'd find a way to layer in an external flourish. There is a beauty to it, for some."

I spotted the repeating pattern and managed to see something new in the building I had missed. I had walked along the side of this building dozens of times for different appointments and only absentmindedly glanced at the concrete design, which to me felt dated and excessive. But as I saw Michael run his fingers over the concrete patterns, I recognized that Stone had a cunning imagination and wanted this building to dazzle, at least for the public and visitors.

But when we walked inside, my stomach tightened. The ceilings were low and stifling. Fluorescent bulbs lit the drab hallways, making our complexions a mix of hollow, pale, and pitiful. Michael went searching for the map, which was harder to find. But eventually he located it, and we stared at a case study in chaos. Darting lines and abrupt ends. A labyrinth lacking a decipherable story.

I sighed.

"So, part of the problem here is that it's clear the hospital had to keep making additions—whole wings, and then a series of carve-outs here and there—to accommodate the need. So, what Stone put in motion—which initially had a sense of beauty, although it wasn't patient-centered—is now more of a functional but jumbled series of amendments to his design. It really is tough to see," Michael said. "But, of course, no one meant any harm. This is common in older hospitals all over the world."

Patient-centered. I remember that's how Visser described Colocci to me in our first conversation.

We strolled by the waiting area where months ago Sebastien had chosen to pull a chair and sit across from me rather than join me on the couch. I took a seat while Michael inspected the ceilings, and I heard him say something about how the interior ventilation system offered a clue about how the ad hoc additions took shape.

But my mind was squarely centered in the terrible waiting area. The uncomfortable couch, the chairs that weren't meant to move. How I knew then that Sebastien understood ominous news was drawing ever closer. How he always knew. How he likely knew far more even today than he felt comfortable telling me.

After only about twenty minutes inside the old hospital, I could feel my general sense of abiding hope draining, and I wanted out. "Ready to go?" I asked Michael.

"Sure. I think we've seen enough."

Loveliness matters. I've always known this, but only in the last room have I come to understand why. Loveliness—this notion of bringing an intentional sweetness, a goodness, an elegant and yet forever accessible beauty—smooths the inevitable harsh edges.

Loveliness is not flawlessness. Once, as Don and I gasped for air as we drowned in the sorrows of infidelity, he said a truism—*I never said I was perfect.* I was gutted. He didn't intend to hurt me with such a seemingly innocuous reminder, but it landed with a searing sting.

Perfection is an impossible destination. Moreover, there's no discovery or growth or surprise in perfection—what we crave is a drawing closer toward goodness. A sense that our spouse, or a team of architects, has an imagination for the best-possible outcomes. Most of the time those outcomes will come with fascinating flaws, flaws that form moments that shape a path toward improvement, a continuous yearning for creating ever more joy. As we commit ourselves to those we adore, loveliness emerges alongside the uneven realities of our humanness. To see loveliness, we must embrace an imagination to discover it. This is captivation. A daring to pause and then to receive the wonder, even with—*maybe because of*—the inevitable imperfections.

The last room depends on this. Without loveliness—and eyes to gaze upon it—the last room collapses and becomes a rubble of randomness. Loveliness comes from intentional design, and perhaps that's why Paul included this virtue when writing from his own last room. Maybe Paul understood—as I was just beginning to grasp—that loveliness is a covenant: an agreement that the sunrise from my hospital window and the taste of summer strawberries paired with a sweet yellow cake and a walk-off home run and the peace that comes in a lover's embrace are all moments when we glimpse our true selves. Telling reminders of who we know we can be, yearn to be, and sometimes are.

Driving away from the hospital, I glanced over at an adjacent building, where Visser meets with his patients. I hadn't seen him in months. Now the focus was on my lungs; at the stoplight I concluded there was a decent chance our paths wouldn't cross again. I wondered what kinds of patients he might be seeing that day and whether he was describing the same playbook he had given me back in July 2019.

I envisioned him wearing one of his impeccable suits, and after my conversation with Michael, I began to see something more at work. I had been charmed from the beginning by Visser's suits, but I had always assumed, well, he must have had an important hospital administrator to see or maybe he was speaking at a conference or there was probably a board meeting right after my appointment.

His suits were about none of that. I had seen him in too many settings, and every single time he came dressed with such care and purposefulness. His suits said this: *You matter. You are my patient and you matter so much that I will show you by dressing with care and respect. Some doctors might call this form of consideration outdated, and if that's true for them, they better show up for their patients with whatever form of respect they have to bring. As for me, I will show you how important our conversation is by dressing in a way that shows how genuinely I care.*

I finally understood it. I adored it. I found within his beautiful suits a new dimension to this ever-expanding word *lovely.* Visser brought a profound intentionality to his appointments by dressing as if it were the most important meeting of his year, because it was. Like the new Stanford hospital, I came to see his suits as a way of expressing a patient-centered priority. Through an atrium's architectural design that created an abundance of light and a physician's carefully selected ties, I discovered a joyful deliberateness, something loveliness requires to endure.

I also learned there's a step before. Bringing intentionality to a person or a community hinges on a radical commitment to knowing who you're creating loveliness for. If an architect is going to embark on a journey creating a hospital that will enable a sense of healing for patients, she must commit herself fully to discovering the intricacies of what's beneficial and what might be harmful. There is study involved here, curiosity, and an abiding humility—the kind of humility that opens a window to see what was once overlooked, designing with an eye toward enduring purpose rather than short-term accolades.

It all begins with paying attention.

A year before I was diagnosed, Connor and I were in Chicago with an open afternoon. I suggested we be like Ferris Bueller and witness the best the city had to offer on that spring day. Connor asked me who Ferris Bueller was.

We had about three hours to work with, so I assured him that when we got home we'd make a date to watch one of the best films of all time, but for now we'd saunter over to Chicago's Art Institute and take in as much beauty as we could find before the museum closed.

We bought our tickets and then realized we had only a little more than an hour until the museum closed. We talked through our plan: a tip of the cap to Seurat, Caillebotte, Monet, Cassatt, and Renoir in the Impressionist galleries and then we would center the bulk of our time in the contemporary wing. As we set out, I glanced over to where the museum staff seemed to be packing up the audio tours for the day.

"Connor, hold up," I said. "Do you think we ought to get audio tours?"

"Well, we don't have a lot of time," he said. "How much are they?"

The man at the desk overhead us, waved us closer, and handed us each a set.

"No charge," he said. "We're nearly closed for the day, so go ahead and take these. Have fun."

Within minutes, we were surrounded by clouds of Impressionist color, surprise, and enchantment. Like nearly all Art Institute patrons, my eyes fixed on Seurat's *A Sunday on La Grande Jatte*, a masterpiece in pointillism in which every dot pulls you closer to the larger scene—harmonies of color working in concert to create a sense of timelessness. The more I gazed, the more I was drawn to a handful of dots that created a little girl wearing a white sundress in the artwork's center, its heart. I thought of Lucy and how she'd worn a dress very much like this one when she was in preschool and how she loved dresses so much she refused to play soccer because the outfit (as she called her uniform) wasn't her style. I had a hard time disagreeing with her.

Connor tapped me on the shoulder. "Mom, let's go. We only have a little time left to see the modern stuff."

We snaked down gallery hallways and upstairs to the contemporary wing, the accessible images replaced by a mix of dissonance and disorientation as we wandered into rooms holding a collection of sculptures, paintings, and objects—some created to stun, some that seemed to poke fun, and others meant to provoke.

We small-talked about the Jackson Pollock we both liked and stared at the de Kooning for long enough to get lost in the swirly white brushstrokes. A collection of found objects affixed to the walls clearly had a place of honor, but we confessed we needed to take more art classes to sort out why. By this time, we had lowered our audio headsets to our necks to exchange amateur "hmms" and "I wonder what this is about?" commentary that revealed that the two of us were clearly out of our depth.

"What do you think is going on with this one?" Connor asked, pointing to a corner of the room.

"Connor, I'm pretty sure that's a fire extinguisher," I said.

"Ahh, yes," he replied as we humbly confronted our limited education in edgy art.

We had one more room to visit, and as we entered, we spotted a pile of rainbow-colored cellophane-wrapped candy spilling out from the far corner. The colors sparkled in the late-day sun, a mountain of sweetness.

"Okay, that's art," Connor said. "See—it says 'Untitled.' So, it must be something."

"Mm-hmm," I said. "It's definitely something," sounding ever more uninformed.

"Well, let's take a listen," Connor said, putting his headset back on.

I followed suit and switched on the device to hear more about this pile of candy.

The narrator's calm and reassuring voice told us about the artist, Félix González-Torres, an American born in Cuba, who created sculpture out of common materials. The work at our feet was a tribute to his partner, who had died of complications from AIDS in 1991. And though the piled candies were dazzling on their own, Connor and I quickly learned that the true magic of this work came from its invitation: patrons were meant to take a candy out of the pile, unwrap it, and savor it. We were meant to eat the art.

We glanced at each other to make sure we both heard all of this correctly, then gingerly bent down to scoop up a candy, unwrap it, and enjoy it.

We learned more.

González-Torres created the work to be 175 pounds, the average weight of a healthy man, and probably the weight of his partner before he became ill. Patrons were invited to participate in the life of the art throughout the day and then, in the evening, museum staff would replenish the candies to return the sculpture to the ideal weight.

We'd never seen, or tasted, anything like it.

Connor leaned down to pick up another candy when we spotted two more gallery visitors wandering through. They glanced at us nervously, then directed a disapproving eye our way, silently telegraphing shame on us for touching the art.

"Mom—they don't know. Should we tell them?"

I turned around and smiled. "Isn't this amazing?" I said. "You should try one—a candy, I mean. That's the point."

They didn't believe me and looked even more troubled.

"No, really," Connor added. "Take one. They're really good candies."

Our fellow patrons looked at us as if we were the kind of people who would mistake a fire extinguisher for art, turned on their heels, and exited the gallery.

"Wow," Connor said, with probably two more candies swirling in his mouth. "Wow, they totally missed it. Too bad. Do you think we should take some for the road?"

"Yeah, let's take one more for our pockets." We strolled out, now convinced of the life-changing power of an audio tour.

It took a long time for me to recognize the invitation of that brief visit to a museum and the awakening by something as seemingly simple as an audio tour. In our curiosity to learn more about the art, we listened. In our listening, we discovered an important story unfolding—one far more expansive than our own assumptions and biases. In our reckoning, Connor and I found a form of enchantment in our own humility, our recognition that we were now part of a narrative that transcended our limited vantage points. Mostly this: we learned what González-Torres was trying to tell us because we listened and then participated. Our story became connected to the artist's, to his beloved's, and to all patrons who discovered how to honor both fragility and fortitude.

An audio tour revealed the story as it was rather than the story we thought we knew. The audio tour brought us closer to the truth, a telling reminder that when the lights of my last room would glow together, they created a luminous space.

Visser's suits revealed respect, devotion, humility.

Stanford's new hospital revealed a standard of excellence—architects who devoted both time and imagination to studying centuries of hospital architecture and patient testimonials to make a space centered on healing.

All three created delight, an eternal reminder that our hearts desire enchantment. The philosopher Simone Weil said it this way: *The longing to love beauty of the world... is essentially the longing for the incarnation.*

Those flourishes of beauty are a gift for our here and now and a telling reminder that our longings are in service to a broader set of possibilities. An embrace of wonder, a faith that the beauty we get to glimpse in all the rooms of our lives may be a foreshadowing for what's to come.

This is why loveliness is magical.

Whatever Is Admirable

If you carefully read the fine print in the brochures advertising life on Planet Cancer, you'll discover an important disclaimer about the rhythm of scans. They dictate everything.

Most days, many of us who live on this planet move gracefully about—seemingly looking fine—carrying a quiet knowing about the next scan. We can tell you when it will be, how life might shift after the images are analyzed, how days leading up to a scan feel suspended. We might mention how important it is to resist the pull of suspension and choose instead to live fully even while our futures hang precariously in the balance. We will whisper how continuing is far more courageous than surrendering to a scan's temptations to question whether any of these days in between the images matter at all.

If you listen carefully, we'll tell you how emotionally exhausting it is to live scan to scan. To know that it matters not if our remaining hair is shiny or our lashes are full, but rather what our insides look like when rendered in black and white.

The images are white specs—shifting shapes, like clouds—that reveal truth: we're not like you at all. Our bodies are broken. Our bodies need help. Our bodies are heroically working to heal.

As a practical matter, my scans happened about every ninety days. Those who are on a six- or twelve-month cadence are in a relatively more stable place. Those in the ninety-day club live with constant uncertainty and hope. Another duality familiar to last-room dwellers, but a space nearly impossible to describe to those looking in the last room's windows and wondering how it's all going for us.

My August 2020 scan was blissfully boring, so Ko and Colocci agreed it was time for me to lower the dose of a maintenance chemo—pills I would take with breakfast and dinner. The main side effects were lingering exhaustion and something new and odd: I kept losing skin on my hands and feet. I mitigated it by constantly lathering my skin with lotion that was more like Vaseline, and it felt like an easy price to pay for keeping the disease at bay.

This maintenance time coincided with the start of the most unconventional school year in the history of modern schooling. Connor and Lucy started their senior and sophomore years in their bedrooms, laptops open. The first day was charming. They had both gotten up early, groomed, and found first-day-of-school outfits that were camera-ready. I took the obligatory first-day-of-school pictures while they begged me to get out of their bedrooms, and we all acknowledged the absurdity of it all.

It took about four days for the charm to deteriorate into churn. Camera-ready morning hair became camera-off bedhead. Hours would go by with my children holed up in their bedrooms while I Zoomed downstairs, and I would wonder whether they were still alive up there, behind their closed doors. Occasionally, I would peek in to find a grumpy teenager, still in bed, listening to a chemistry lecture, sort of.

Pajamas became okay to wear at three o'clock in the afternoon, and there was nothing I could do about that.

I knew when Connor was in his statistics class because this was when he would riff on his ukulele. In his pajamas.

Lucy mentioned that her English teacher insisted that everyone in class at least put a picture of themselves up on their Zoom profile if they elected to keep their camera off. The next day everyone in the class had picked out baby pics; I glanced over her shoulder one morning while she was in AP English only to see twenty-four tiles of toddlers.

Can I tell you which high school class doesn't work on Zoom? Tuesdays and Thursdays at ten o'clock, Connor's trumpet would burst into song for his advanced jazz class. Can we all pause for a moment and consider the hundreds of thousands of music teachers who attempted to teach their young students who were sitting at home with their horns and flutes and bassoons in their bedrooms, in Zoom boxes, and most likely in their pajamas?

We were all slowly losing our minds.

Late nights and into the early mornings, I silently doom scrolled, scanning county COVID numbers and comparing them with national trends. I was desperate to live normally again, knowing this little season of stability likely wouldn't last.

One September day, determined to reclaim what used to be a Saturday routine, I decided to go on a familiar hike—a five-mile loop with a steep ascent. I felt fine-ish. Fine, but diminished. Fine, but fatigued.

It was a warm day and I breathed heavily about two and half miles in. We all wore masks then, even outside, but I kept mine below my chin when no one was around. It was getting harder to breathe on the path and I was increasingly frustrated by how unfamiliar my once-familiar hike felt after enduring so much chemo and two surgeries. I stopped, let others pass me, and took a long drink from my water bottle. I kept climbing and then felt flushed. The sun was intense while I steadied my feet—why was I losing my balance? Then, an awful wave of nausea took hold, a sensation strangely brand new. Through all of that chemo, I had never once thrown up, but now, on the trail, it was inevitable.

I quickly looked around, relieved not to see any other hikers, found a tree, and emptied my stomach at its base. My hands were shaking as I reached for more water and wondered whether it might be faster to turn around or continue on. I was almost at the summit, and the nausea passed as quickly as it had arrived, so I kept going. But I was mortified. What if someone had seen me, or heard me, retching? Would they assume I had some terrible case of COVID and scream at me for infecting their mountain air? But it was more than that—I was scared. What was happening?

This was new. Did it mean something terrible was in motion? And why was I hiking alone?

By the time I made my way to the descent, my feet were on fire. My skin was slowly healing from the onslaught of blisters, but I had underestimated how tender it was. The last half mile at the base of the hill, on the long path back to my car, I hobbled. The last hundred yards I managed to walk on my tiptoes, knowing any more weight on the balls of my feet would result in agony.

Finally, I climbed into the front seat, carefully took off my tennis shoes, then my socks, and stared at my swollen, bright-red feet. They throbbed in anger at me for daring such a long trek with such fragile skin.

My heart pinballed from gratitude—*Who would have thought a year ago I'd be here!*—to brutal despair—*How on earth did I end up in such a mess?* I was alive!—hiking more than five miles—and I was frail.

Seldom did I have a thought that didn't reside on the edges of extreme. I'd spot a hummingbird outside my living room window and marvel at her as long as she'd hover. The next second, I'd glance at a medical bill on my counter and the marvel would dive into a dark sorrow. If there was an emotional in-between, I didn't know when I would find my way back to it.

Meanwhile, I'd stopped flossing. This happened gradually. I'd skip the weekends and then give myself a flossing hall pass every other night. Then I decided I was all in: Who on earth needs to floss in their last room? I'd always hated it. And now the idea of enduring the torture as some kind of investment to pay off in my seventies seemed laughable. Like an easy hassle I could happily abandon. To be clear, I didn't completely abandon the dental ship. That little water pick device that came with my electric toothbrush became my last-room permission slip allowing me to trust that my gums would be just fine for my last-room existence.

In fact, the more time I spent in the last room, the more I began to dabble with shedding anything that was an unnecessary bother. There was a time in my life when I would carefully hand-wash some high-end knives that Don and I had bought; the salesperson had told me that hand-washing was the best way to preserve them for decades. After my diagnosis, I threw them in the dishwasher with zero hesitation (and they have held up just fine).

As I shed such small things, I grew to appreciate graceful exits that held more consequence. Banter with friends that tilted toward fun gossip became less entertaining. I developed a far better set of instincts about how to shift a conversation that could be headed toward unintended harm, mainly because I was so exhausted by harm.

My days became liberated, with a continuous pull toward goodness. And on my best days, I found ways to set goodness in motion.

That cliché question we've all passed around the dinner table—*What would you do if you had only a year or two left to live?*—I was answering it, in real time. And my answer astonished me:

solidly 80 percent of my normal days were spent doing exactly what I'd want to be doing if I was down to my last twenty-four months.

While working with my team at Emerson to build a new cohort of fellows—individuals who hailed from vastly different disciplines who were working at the intersection of COVID recovery and racial justice reckonings—I was riveted daily. Our applicants described projects that were as innovative as they were urgent.

I discovered the joy of tipping extra. Bumping 20 percent to 30 percent for the server or the Door Dasher became an easy way to sprinkle a little joy in my wake.

I embraced a deeper bias toward yes.

And I think we all know where a bias toward yes in the last room leads: a puppy.

Lucy had been making the case for a dog since she was old enough to make a case. In the flurry of the move to Menlo Park and the divorce, I fully admit I soothed the occasional awful day with vague big talk about a dog... *someday*. The problem with vague big talk in the company of a ten-year-old girl is that ten-year-old girls have a way of keeping track. Of keeping score. Of reminding you that vague big talk sounds an awful lot like a contract, and people who break contracts with young girls are more like Putin than moms who profess to love their daughters.

Every year that passed dogless, Lucy's belief in my vague big talk about a fictional dog downgraded to skepticism. By the time she was a teenager, she wasn't wrong to remind me that I was a walking failure in the "maybe next year will be the Year of the Dog" department.

But here in the last room, I began to envision long walks with a dog. A cute puppy that would lick our noses and curl up next us.

One summer a few years earlier, the kids and I had visited my dear friend Ann, who lived on Maryland's Eastern Shore with her sweet Cavalier King Charles Spaniel, Peachy. Peachy was a ruby Cavvy, which meant her coat was a rich hue of browns and reds and golds—perfection on four paws.

So, did I print out a picture of a ruby Cavvy and surround that picture with the most fabulous happy birthday letter to my dear Lucy, with an ironclad promise that some version of a Peachy puppy would be ours . . . for reals? Oh, you bet your last room I did.

Lucy squealed with delight. And I made a call to Ann.

"Hello! Hi! I'm calling with a question for you."

"Oh, hello! Wait, first tell me how you're doing."

"Right—yes, okay. Well. Here's the thing. I feel great! And I'm in such a precarious spot. I'm not sick, but I'm not well. Scan in a few weeks, so who knows what will come next. Constant joy and uncertainty here!"

We spent thirty minutes settling into my ridiculousness, deeply familiar to me and jarring to any friend who dared ask a follow-up question.

I then found a way to segue to puppy small talk and asked about how I might go about finding a Peachy of my own. Ann grew up in North Carolina, and she had a gentle drawl that makes her words sound like lyrical mint julep.

"Oh, *honey*," she declared. "Rubies are *rare*."

"Oh, gosh, really? How did you get Peachy?"

"We were on a list. My son had to fly to Kansas to pick her up. This will be *a process*."

Lord have mercy. Who has time for a puppy process in the last room?

I got to googling and discovered a Cavvy breeder about two hours from our house. The puppies on her website were a mix of black and tans, with an occasional ruby puppy face tucked into frolicking cuteness.

When I expressed my desire to adopt a ruby, this breeder said, "Cavvies are special dogs. And they are in high demand."

"I bet," I said. I then did what all of us on Planet Cancer sometimes do: I played my hand. "You see, several months ago I was diagnosed with stage IV cancer. No symptoms! No family history! Just whammy." I eased into telling my tale with just the right mix of tenderness and hopefulness, all the while hearing occasional barking in Pam's background. Then I readied my dismount. "So, I think you'd agree, Pam, this is the *ideal* time for my daughter and me to welcome a ruby into our home. We're just so eager to love, now more than ever."

Pam was quiet while the dogs in her house were not. "Right, okay," she said. "As I mentioned, these dogs are in high demand. The current litter is spoken for, but in about six months I may have another. I'm happy to put you on the waiting list for that litter, but it's important I meet my prospective Cavvy parents before that happens."

"Before the waiting list for the litter six months away happens?" I asked.

"Yes," Pam said.

"Oh," I said, realizing that I didn't have another card to play. "Well. Hmm. We'd of course love to meet you," I said, banking on the idea that perhaps in-person charm might bump us up from waiting list to sure thing.

"Sure," she said. "But I do need to ask, and I'm sorry if this sounds a little, well, indelicate."

"Oh, gosh, ask anything," I said.

"Well. You know I place my puppies in forever homes. And, uh, I'm just curious. I mean, given your situation, do you have, um, a plan? I mean, for when, you know... It's just important that I know from the outset that the puppy will have a place to go for when, I guess, you're gone."

This was a new one. I had thought through every kind of contingency for the kids if the next scan was a dumpster fire—how important it would be for Don to move to Menlo so they could finish high school with their friends, their financial needs, Jacquelline's plan to surround them with a chorus of smart wisdom and advice givers—but I freely admit I had not given even a second's thought to what would happen to a puppy if I departed the stage prematurely.

"Oh, gosh," I said. "Well, we never would have considered this awesome responsibility without thinking through every kind of scenario." I paused. "And, of course, this will be my daughter's dog, and my daughter is in excellent health."

"But how old did you say she is? She's going to college relatively soon, yes?"

"Yes. But the wonderful thing is that Lucy's father is deeply devoted, and he happens to adore dogs too. If the worst-possible thing happens, this puppy will have a loving home with Lucy, and while she's in college I'm sure she'll be able to see the dog all the time at her dad's house."

More quiet, except for dogs barking. I'm fairly sure Pam was wondering if she would need to meet Don before we could qualify for her waiting list.

"So, Pam. How about Lucy and I stop by in the next week or so to say hello?"

"Okay, sure," she said, still sounding hesitant. "The most recent litter is here and there is one ruby in the bunch, so you and your daughter can meet her, which is always a treat. Mind you, this ruby was paired with a forever home a few months ago, but still, it's a treat."

I kept Ann updated; she laughed and promised to pray for a puppy miracle. Two weeks later, Lucy and I drove two hours to meet some puppies, a drive that coincided with my discovery that it's possible to listen to Taylor Swift on a four-hour round-trip road trip without one song repeated.

We knocked on the door and were greeted by a joyous herd of Cavvies. It was as if this was the first time they'd met a human, and they were determined to shower us with love because we deserved nothing but love.

And then, from the joyous herd of adult Cavvies and baby Cavvies emerged a little sparkle of a ruby puppy, who tilted her head just so, as if to say, "Oh, hello. You two are so very beautiful and I was put on this planet to love you and sit next to you and remind you every day that today is the best day ever, even better than yesterday, which up until then was also the best day ever."

Lucy and I found a spot on the couch, and Pam scooped up this baby ruby Cavvy and placed her in Lucy's arms. I'd love to regale you with tales of thoughtful questions and compliments we gave Pam about her beautiful dogs and puppies, but there's simply no time. Instead, all you need to know is that we devolved into a mess of "SHE IS THE MOST ADORABLE CREATURE THIS PLANET HAS EVER PRODUCED" and were more or less done for.

Pam cautiously interrupted our waterfall of cooing and gushing to provide a bit of breaking news. "So, this is all so interesting. Just last night the woman who had picked out this puppy called to say that she was thinking now she wanted a black and tan. This is highly unusual. And also, poor form. All of these puppies are beautiful and I'm not sure how I feel about such an eleventh-hour change of heart about a puppy's coat."

Lucy and I exchanged glances, knowing we were born for this moment. For this couch. As she cradled Ms. Most Perfect Creature in the History of Earth in her arms, Lucy looked up with her big blue eyes and said, "Well, that's just so hard to believe. It's really all about love, isn't it? I mean, we're all here to simply give and receive love. All I know is that this puppy deserves as much love as possible."

I, stroking Ms. Most Perfect's sweet head, came in strong as Lucy's wingwoman. "We also believe—so very deeply—in safety. What I mean by that is, all puppies need to live in a safe and secure home. A home with a back area with plenty of space to trot about and one with a secure gate. We also love to play. Oh, how much do we love to play! Is there anything better than seeing all those well-behaved pooches near our house romp around at the dog park. No. In fact there is nothing better."

We kept it up for forty-five minutes and by the time we left we were the proud owners of a Cavvy with a ruby coat, who would come home with us in two weeks' time.

We settled into the car, slightly stunned by what had just transpired.

"First of all," Lucy said, "Ann is one hell of a prayer."

"I know it," I said, beginning to do the math for what we'd be spending soon at Petco, a vet, and other line items I then knew nothing about.

"And second," Lucy said, "let's call her Bonnie."

"Bonnie is perfect," I said.

Bonnie joined our little family and exceeded our wildest expectations of cuteness. I carefully set up her crate in Lucy's room and reminded her that those first few nights Bonnie might whimper here and there, but as long as she soothed her with a comforting voice and reminded her that she was so very close by, the puppy would be just fine.

Later that night, Lucy crept into my room with the crate and said it would be better if Bonnie slept with me. "She's a little noisy and I think she feels safer with you." She carefully placed the crate next to my bed while I drowsily muttered, "—wait, what?"

"Okay, sweet Bonnie. You'll love it here," Lucy whispered. And then to me, "See, Mom? She's quieted down already. Okay, good night, you two!" And there it was. A ten-year lobbying campaign for a puppy to call her own boomeranged back to me in less than ten hours.

The last room now had a full-time puppy who was never more than a step behind me. Bonnie was most welcome.

But even with the world's most adorable puppy following me everywhere, I couldn't shake a growing sense of dread. By this point—chemo, abdominal surgery, chemo, lung surgery, maintenance chemo—I had my choice of places to scan and which physician would walk me through the results. I'd scheduled the scan this time for Stanford medical center, in part because I had learned that if I scheduled it for a Friday morning, I could also arrange time with Visser on that same day, which meant that my results would be delivered to me in person, like in the movies. Data getting pushed to your phone has its place, but for this scan, I wanted to have a proper chat. With a surgeon in a suit.

By two o'clock that day, I was perched on the table in Visser's exam room. The nurse took my vitals and complimented me on my blood pressure numbers.

Then, the gap. The time in-between seeing the nurse and the doctor. An empty room, the crinkling paper on the exam table, the otherwise unrelenting quiet.

Enjoy the peace, I told myself. *You never get an uninterrupted fifteen minutes to simply breathe.*

Enjoy this?! There is no peace here. There is only terror.

Phone scrolling. Lame.

Peace, terror, peace, terror.

I'd had enough practice with pattern recognition over the past year and a half to know that a gap of more than twenty minutes in an exam room meant one of two things: (1) the patient before you was in a complicated space and required far more time than scheduled, or (2) your scan needed a closer look, and a big breath, before news was delivered.

Finally, Visser entered, with a resident in tow. Charcoal-gray suit, sky-blue tie with a bold yellow diagonal stripe. Slumped shoulders. And a long sigh. I wanted to turn off my ears.

"So, I'm afraid I've got tough news," he said. "You've got a new slew of lung mets. The disease is back. This is a hard turn. Oh, and you also have a pulmonary embolism, so we need to deal with that too. As I said, this is tough."

I steadied myself on the exam table. "How many mets?" I asked. "How big are they?"

He swiveled on his stool to show me the images on the computer, but he didn't seem all that interested in getting into the minutiae. For Visser, new mets meant this disease still lingered in my body, despite his superb work in my abdomen. The number, the size, all of that were simply supporting details of the terrible headline: I was so beautifully close to emerging from these awful woods, but the forest just revealed itself to be far denser than we had hoped.

He was kind and matter-of-fact. "They're scattered and they're mostly small. I'm sorry about all of this," he said. "I know this is tough. The best thing I can tell you is to get back on chemo, which has worked for you before. Oh, and we'll put you on a blood thinner, too, for the embolism."

Visser and I had arrived at a new place. We didn't speak of playbooks, of a way forward. Instead, we looked at each other knowing that his role on my stage was likely coming to a close. His character in this drama was equal parts devoted, candid, kind, and talented, but he no longer had any lines in the script.

"Yes, okay," I said. "How bananas is it that I feel so completely fine? I mean, I haven't felt this well in so long."

He rubbed his brow, and I saw his heartbreak, sitting there on the exam-room swivel stool. Eye level, just like lovely Dr. Chen. I think he had seen a survivor in me, but that glimmer faded when he glanced back at the small, cloudy specks on the computer screen.

He made no mention of the mets being schmaltzies.

When I mentioned that I'd stopped flossing, I also meant that I gave myself permission to see if there was a way to reimagine my friendship with Sebastien.

A word here to future last-room dwellers: The last thing we want to do in the last room is start firing people. Trust me on this. Instead, we want to hold on to everyone for dear life. Because we'll realize more than ever before how very dear life is.

The last room has disorienting corners. I'd left Tahoe devasted, humiliated, and mortified that I might have inadvertently played a role in a betrayal. That particular wing of panic subsided as I assured myself there was no equivalency between my marriage and whatever relationship Sebastien had in place with someone else: they were not married, they did not live in the same city, he never once spoke of her to me. Still, if I remained in an unusual friendship with compartmentalized components, I wondered if I was lowering my own standards for what makes for a truthful relationship.

Mental whispers taunted and tempted me.

Sebastien can stay in your life. He's become one of your closest friends. You're adults and you can figure this out.

He's been more devoted to your care than anyone. Unusual circumstances create unusual friendships. Be grateful for his remarkable wisdom and generosity. And his unparalleled connections.

We're living through a pandemic. We're all losing our minds, remember? It's completely fine if you give yourself permission to stay connected to a man who was a little reckless with you.

This is the last room—chances for romance in any form rarely exist here. If you cross a line or two, enjoy yourself while you can.

The taunting whispers were countered by steady reminders that my heart was in no place to sustain additional wounds.

Keeping any kind of friendship alive with him would only lead to a realm where devotion and companionship came with an awful price: romantic dalliance followed by rejection casually cloaked as the collateral damage that's part of the package deal that comes in the last room.

And yet the last room is achingly lonely. There's little chance to begin something new when you reside within an ending.

So, I began to gingerly reopen lines to Sebastien. Depending on my mood, I would respond to texts and then send some of my own. We went on pandemic walks, settling back into our familiar conversational dance: we rarely spoke of relationships with others, choosing instead to live inside our own friendship. In my mind, when I spent time with Sebastien it was like visiting Fiji. It wasn't clandestine. It was simply far away and just disconnected enough that lots of life could be lived without the rest of the globe needing to know much about it.

The more time I spent in the last room, the more time I craved mini vacations from it; Sebastien's friendship became an emotional getaway.

But when the harsh edges of the last room crashed in, my emotional-getaway friend instantly transformed into the most knowledgeable person to interpret the specifics around how harsh the edges were becoming.

So, after texting my family with the distressing turn, I called Sebastien to ask him all the questions I'd neglected to bring to

Visser. He let me know that he'd already been in touch with Visser after I had frantically texted him from the exam room, so he was up to speed on the images. From the first days of my diagnosis, I had given Sebastien full permission to discuss my case with anyone, so I was grateful he had reached out to Visser on my behalf.

"Okay, so first, I know this is a setback, but I see some elements here that are a little reassuring," he began. "The mets seem contained to familiar lines that were there before, which basically means this isn't a massive expansion of disease. And there's no indication of mets anywhere else. These are all very positive dynamics," he said.

I was quiet. I knew that Sebastien was always careful with his words, so he wouldn't mischaracterize the facts at hand. But he could also describe a set of realities while neglecting to characterize their probable consequence. I remembered Visser's slumped shoulders, knowing that although Sebastien's take was accurate, he was carefully hedging on its implications.

"Okay, thanks. This is reassuring, or at least a little comforting. It's still so hard to absorb, though."

"I know. But, remember, you tolerate chemo better than just about any patient I've ever encountered. And these drugs work. Let them work again."

There are two standard chemotherapy regimens for colon cancer: FOLFOX and FOLFIRI. Some patients receive them as a combination, and others (like me) move from one to the other. Each comes with distinct side effects, and each is equally effective. FOLFOX—Foxy—has side effects that include neuropathy in the hands and feet, which can be debilitating. For me, the neuropathy was hard, at times, but more hassle than horror show. Foxy's big advantage is that hair usually thins some, but not in a way that's too noticeable. FOLFIRI can be harder on the gut—some patients experience more nausea and other unpleasantness. But classic chemo hair loss is the real kicker with FOLFIRI, and ever since my diagnosis I had dreaded this looming drug.

Because I had already completed thirteen rounds of FOLFOX, Ko and Colocci agreed I needed to pivot to FOLFIRI. Ko was kind about it. "I'm sorry about this. You do have lovely hair."

In Paul's letter to his beloveds in Philippi, he prefaces the virtues with a soft encouragement to not just ponder them but also to embrace them. One translation unspools part of this section of his letter this way: "If you believe in goodness and if you value the approval of God, fix your minds on the things which are holy and right."

As I prepared to lose my hair, I wondered whether Paul had a series of surrenders in his own last room; he may not have gone starkly bald, but he likely endured a cascade of losses of dignity while toiling in a Roman jail. And yet during a season of loss, Paul encouraged his friends to anchor. To take on. To fill. To fix their minds on things that were holy and right.

From the first day of my diagnosis, I'd experienced a waterfall of texts, emails, handwritten letters, long phone calls, and even longer walks as each one of my own beloveds shared how they were pulling for me. Me being a bridge dweller, these posts from friends who subscribed to a vast array of ideologies came in a variety of flavors:

> *When I meditate each morning, know that I'm holding you in my heart.*
>
> *I'm praying for you. So is my entire church. You're on the list!*
>
> *Sending good vibes your way.*
>
> *Pulling for you! You're in my thoughts.*
>
> *I'm sending you light today.*
>
> *I pray for you that God would remove those mets. How many are there again? My prayers are specific. Please do keep me posted.*

I received them all as miracles. A vibe, a thought, a well-wish—they were all prayers. Each one sacred. Each one mattered.

But were the prayers being answered? It's an eternal question, and one without an easy answer. Growing up, I found some Christian clichés about prayer—*If you're faithful enough, God will honor your requests!*—ridiculous. As I stepped into adulthood and my view of the world continued to expand, I found those clichés even more problematic. They were insulting and harmful.

The more dire my health became, the more I cherished every form of prayer, and the more I learned to reimagine how—*or if*—those prayers were being answered.

I lost my hair on Good Friday. Most of the nurses in the oncology unit had told me it would likely begin to fall out after the third or fourth round of FOLFIRI, so I knew I was in the inevitable and awful window. But it happened faster than I'd imagined. After a long shower, I tried to comb through my hair, taking extreme care with each strand. But it was no use—my long and once-beautiful hair was a tangled mess of thick mats. One small tug and gobs of hair hit the tiles.

I cried on my bathroom floor and then curled up on my bed for a while. And then put on a baseball cap and kept crying, lacerated by thoughts like,

You knew this was part of the trek. Be brave.
Millions of others have done this. Stop being so vain.
You had such lovely hair. Let's be honest—it was your best feature. And now it's gone.

As I gasped for breath between sobs, softer thoughts and reminders ventured in:

You're still lovely. You are.
You're ready for this.
You'll save a fortune on blowouts.

Each side spoke to me with equal vehemence—and venom—until I could crawl back into bed. But sleep that night took a long while. I spent much of the night in prayer, laments that poured out as meandering pleas for help alongside acknowledgments of the persistent miracles that deserved my gratitude.

Another duality—grief and gratitude, each enveloped by the most generous outpouring of support through well-wishes and prayers.

As I repositioned the baseball cap I slept in those first few nights, I came to realize: it's not about whether prayer works, who we pray to, or even what we call "prayer"; it's about who we become when we fill our minds with holy requests and holy expressions of thanks.

When we pray on behalf of someone else, when we send our warmest thoughts, we venture ever closer to another soul's steps. Even if for a moment, we walk alongside. A prayer says these uncertain steps can be made steadier with a hand to hold.

What's more, in his last room, Paul pleaded for prayer because he knew the act itself is a miraculous anchor of connection. When he wrote "fix your minds," Paul was imploring his friends to replenish, to center. Our minds are constantly active; thoughts beckon our every minute. Throughout his letter to Philippi, Paul invited his dear friends to harness their wonder to a domain of interconnected accord. To a story far more mysterious than we can decipher in the moment.

In other words, Paul asked for and gave prayers to purposefully weave them into a tapestry where every thread matters, even if we cannot yet see how. A tapestry where we all meet each other.

See, prayer didn't release Paul from his Roman jail, but it did open his heart to the mystery of the story unfolding around him. To a richer confidence that, despite the cruelty and pain, a more expansive narrative was in motion.

And yet. For reasons I'll never quite understand, somehow we receive glimpses of prayer's work even as the threads twine in a tapestry often too complex for us to see in its entirety. These glimpses are gifts: a legion of scientists' dedication that turned mustard gas into chemotherapy, Visser's steady hands, Tracy's precious unborn baby who was deemed a lost cause, a friend who flies across the country to sit with me on a scan day, a puppy. A COVID vaccine that saved millions of lives.

Why not more glimpses? Why a puppy and not a cure? Maybe this is the most mysterious part of prayer. Perhaps it's because the tapestry being woven is both far more microscopically intricate and enormously generational than I could ever fathom. Maybe it's because there's a designed mystery unfolding around a grander sequence of events, even as we pray for the story we crave.

Here is what the last room has revealed to me about the way I pray: When I enter into the activity of prayer, I am committing myself to a request having no idea at all if the plea will have the impact I seek. I trust that it might. But it's the persistence of prayer throughout the unknowns that reinforces resilience and hope, and that's what makes it admirable.

Here is why I know. Although this embrace of a more expansive story hasn't healed my body or stopped Putin's madness, it has vacated the most terrifying element of all within the last room: randomness. The dark and icy shadows where plot details lack purpose.

There's more. The months following surgery—the season when I came to fully embrace Don for all of his goodness—I discovered a genuine shift had taken place in my heart. When his name appeared on my phone for a call, instead of bristling, I felt compassion and gratitude. We'd talk about the latest scan and the kids and how to think about the uncertainty facing us all. I could hear the love in his voice—the love I once cherished more than anything—and I received it as a reimagined allyship. Before my heart changed, I clung to a limited form of forgiveness because I mistakenly thought I would be erased from my own story. Instead, I discovered I was released from the prison I had built for myself. I still carried the wounds, but I carried them in a transformed way: I viewed them as elements I was taking with me on a long path toward healing. No longer were they festering and fearful wounds that inhibited any step forward. Prayer surrounded this long and surprising shift. My fears slowly began to subside.

The most common directive in the Bible is an admonishment to be not afraid. When angels showed up to tell the shepherds about the news of Christ's birth, their first words were "Fear not." Throughout the Old Testament, God reminds his people to cast away their fears. Over and over again, Jesus implored his disciples to be brave, to set fear aside. The more prayers I offered up, and the more I received from others, the more I came to see them as sacred dispatches, holy pleas for help, which often eased my fears.

I also came to see that the words *scared* and *sacred* share the same letters. Just one slight inversion, and the entire enterprise pivots. The more sacred the steps, the less scared I became. But why?

Paul knew, as I know now, that there is only one way to diminish the fear that lingers in the shadows of this room—love. If perfect love casts out fear, it means the rooms of our lives are vessels to be filled by the act of turning toward each other.

The turning toward is prayer. It's a drawing closer. It's the art of dwelling alongside—and having the courage to name—the crushing complexity. Prayer is a pledge that says this: your story matters, it has purpose, and I'm here for this chapter and all its bewildering plot twists. It's an invitation to see more than the plot details at hand.

Prayer is a promise you give to another: you're not alone in the last room.

Prayer could very well be the most admirable gift of all.

If Anything Is Excellent

I NEEDED A BREAK.

A break from wrapping this misery package with my carefully designed ribbons of hope that signaled to the kids, and to everyone, *Look, here, I'm a lovely sport.* A break from the smells of the infusion center, a tincture of disinfectant melded with a more subtle scent that I could only describe as exhaustion. A break from walking down the street and seeing couples on first dates or celebrating anniversaries, knowing I no longer belonged to the world of romance. A break from keeping everyone up to speed on my chemo rounds and how I was feeling and how, despite it all, I was in great shape. A break from feeling constantly broken.

I wanted—craved—an eyedropper's worth of delicious living. I wanted to swoosh down a mountainside after gazing at the horizon from the summit, and I wanted to see Sebastien waiting for me at the base of the hill, smiling, with his arms outstretched.

I wanted this knowing my friendship with Sebastien was a jumbled mess of affection, disappointment, hope, medical wisdom, chemistry, and toxic compartmentalization.

One night the prior fall, before Bonnie's arrival in our lives, before chemo and my hair loss, on the heels of my disastrous solo hike, I'd struggled to fall asleep as I played out all the impossible scenarios millions of other single parents face when reckoning with a terminal diagnosis. I needed to get my financial house in order—my will needed to be updated, and I had been advised I should begin the process of setting up trusts for Connor and Lucy with what I had been previously setting aside for retirement.

I knew I needed to get organized, but instead I'd started clicking on websites of resorts in Hawaii, dreaming of a Christmas getaway. Within twenty minutes at two in the morning, I'd confirmed six nights at a five-star resort on the Big Island, smiling at the idea that only in the last room would anyone be that reckless with money. *What's the worst thing that could happen?* I'd asked myself. *I'll live, conclude my career without much in the way of savings, and end up living on a family member's couch? What a fabulous problem to have! Maybe we'll fly first-class to Hawaii.*

Morning came, and as I'd sipped my coffee, I remembered what I'd done the night before. I decided to call a financial planner skilled in these matters to temper my wee-hour last-room splurges.

"You'll need to pick an age," she said.

"An age?" I asked.

"Yes. The age when you think they'll be ready to access the trust. Some parents arbitrarily pick twenty-one. But I have other clients who choose to wait until their offspring are thirty so they can make more mature decisions about their resources. Oh, and you'll want to decide whether or not you'll want to leave your body to science. That's one more decision for when we meet."

I'd stood in my little garden and wondered whether an anatomy class in a couple of years would want a cancerous cadaver to inspect. Was that a thing? There was only one person in my life who would indulge such an odd question.

It had seemed a perfect reason to send an innocent text to Sebastien.

> Oh, hey there. Listen, I need to make all kinds of odd end-of-life decisions because, well, end of life here. Anyhow, do you think an anatomy class would want my body someday even though I've had cancer? I mean, I don't have a gallbladder or a spleen, so maybe that's a dealbreaker?

Sebastien sent a picture of himself and his lab partner back in medical school smiling over their cadaver, whom they'd nicknamed Gladys. And then he went on about how valuable it is to think about science and anatomy with end-of-life matters. He didn't acknowledge my missing gallbladder in the exchange, cleverly nudging the topic away from my gloomy question.

That little text dance led to other topics to sweep our minds out of pandemic doldrums, and I continued to whisper to myself that anyone in the last room would hold on to as many friends as possible. Even one as complicated as Sebastien.

Text exchanges graduated into cautious walks, like the kind we used to take right after I was diagnosed. And because Sebastien hadn't moved to the woman-he-never-spoke-of's hometown, and she wasn't residing in San Francisco, I concluded that maybe their relationship wasn't all that serious.

And once I reached that conclusion, it didn't take long for my exhausted brain to carelessly reason that Sebastien's hesitation over me must be centered on my grim long-term prospects. Maybe he was looking into his crystal ball of all of my scans, and then knowing—more than anyone—*she's probably got eighteen to twenty-four months. Better play it safe!* If that was the case, no one on the planet other than Putin would ever actually put language to that terrible tension: *Listen, Amy, I'm so besotted with you. It's just that, well, you're not long for this world. Can you blame me for hedging on starting anything serious with you?*

If true, this stung. But it also made sense, and I had some detached compassion for it.

Sebastien's hedging hinted at a clue only he carried.

I became semiobsessed with teasing out my odds by monitoring how every element of our Great Relationship Reset would play out. If we were to grow close again, was that a signal that my chances at more years were improving?

I also missed kissing him.

I had tried dating a few other lovely men along the way. Pandemic dates nearly always meant long walks with Bonnie in step, and it was nearly impossible not to talk about health matters given that the entire world was dealing with health matters.

Because I didn't look sick, it was easy for me to layer cancer into the story in a way that likely sounded too casual for some. "Yup, well, I have the kind of cancer that you manage rather than cure. Like a part of my body is on fire, but if you can keep the fire in the fireplace, all is well. I mean, who doesn't love a cozy fire? Anyhow, that's what I'm doing—keeping all those little crackling flames in the fireplace, praying like mad a little ember doesn't dash out and catch a curtain or a couch aflame."

Some stared at me in wonder, mystified by my breezy confidence. Others glanced at me in semihorror, wondering how on earth they ended up on a walk with a woman on fire and the world's cutest dog.

One potential suitor suggested we have an outside dinner instead of a walk, which I thought would be a nice change of pace. It turned out we had all kinds of professional friends in common and other worlds that had a series of uncanny intersections. We realized we had the same taste in *New Yorker* cartoons and opinion columnists and the overconsidered salads we were both enjoying. It was as sweet a date I'd had since before I got sick, and I adored how it all felt to simply spend two hours discovering lily pads of commonality.

We stayed in touch in the days following, flirting over text and an occasional call as we made plans for a second outdoor dinner date.

When the second date night rolled around, I was in my closet sorting out which skirt to wear when my phone pinged with a text.

Hi. Hey, do you have time for a quick FaceTime call?

A 4:00 p.m. text before a date is an ominous sign. I'm certain this is true no matter where you live, no matter your station in life. A nineteen-year-old living in Saigon who gets a 4:00 p.m. pre-date text will hear that ping with the same dread as a sixty-seven-year-old who's wrapping up her day in Salzburg.

Sure. Give me a few minutes, but happy to chat!

I found a spot outside in my garden for the call, wondering why he was insistent about FaceTiming. I applied lip gloss, ready for whatever was incoming.

My phone hummed and I picked up. And there in my small screen was my handsome future dinner date, curled up in an oversized chair in his living room, looking positively disheveled. I wondered if he was hungover, but it was 4:00 p.m. Had he been mugged? Had he been cleaning out his garage when a large critter of some sort leapt from the rafters and somehow landed on his head?

"Hi, there," he said, with a painful grimace. He then started rubbing his brow.

"Oh, hi. Everything okay?" I asked.

"Well. Not really," he said. He looked up to his ceiling, and I swear I caught a tear in his eye. Pure anguish. What on earth was wrong with him?

"Yeah, listen. I need to cancel our date tonight. I've got a pounding migraine. And, well. It's all just... well... too... much. It sucks, though. You're really awesome. I mean, damn. God, you're as good as they come. And now I'm back in touch with someone else, from a while back. I mean who knows about that. But, wow, God this sucks. But, yeah, sorry. I mean, it's all just . . . a lot. Also, my migraines, they happen when I get stressed, so I wanted you to know I wasn't just bullshitting you."

I looked into my phone, watching a grown man spinning with anguish and rambling apologies cloaked in an odd mix of pity and relief.

"Oh, gosh! Wow. I totally get it. And holy cow. I think this is the first time I've ever given someone a migraine. Geez. Well, it would have been lovely getting to know you, but I get it! Listen, be well. All good!"

"You're so cool. Thanks. Sorry, again," he said, wincing and rubbing his brow.

I hung up. I stared at Bonnie. I was now making men physically sick at the thought of dating me.

The last room was a dumpster fire of lame.

The absurdity of it all naturally had a way of lowering my personal stakes. I realized my migraine-suffering FaceTimer was living the long game. He was looking for a love that would last for decades. I was, too, but most likely my love story could last only months. Who wouldn't end up with a migraine when confronted with that kind of dichotomy?

Each day that passed—feeling physically well but knowing my odds at longevity stayed persistently grim—I crept ever closer to adopting a new mental framework.

I was now playing the short game in a long-game world.

Growing up, my dad spent a good deal of time with me and my brother and sister teaching us different sports—he instilled in each of us a love of tennis, golf, and baseball. My dad understood that what made these particular sports so exceptional was that the clock didn't determine the final score. Each serve, drive, and at bat was a chance to reset the game. Hope was always in play and always on deck. I once lost a first tennis set 1–6 and came back to beat my high school opponent 7–5 and then also won the tiebreaker. We stayed out on that court for more than two hours, and I reveled in the notion that no buzzer would sound to arbitrarily end the match.

Growing up in San Diego and rooting for the Padres, my brother and sister and I knew a little something about hope. We'd earned PhDs in hope. Most years, the Padres were out of contention by Mother's Day, but still we scrambled to get to games, pinning all of our dreams on Tony Gwynn and remembering that miracles had a way of showing up despite it all. With a stirring in our hearts, we'd sit in the cheap seats, so high I thought we were closer to touching the moon than the field. What might happen?

Usually, not much. But we kept piling into the station wagon to go to games, season after season.

In the 1986 Masters, Jack Nicklaus—who held sainthood status in our home—was behind Greg Norman as they entered the final round. Nicklaus steadily made eight pars in a row and then decided to astonish the fans at Augusta by shooting six-under par to triumph over Norman in the back nine, winning by one stroke. I was fifteen and knew I was bearing witness to why my dad so loved golf: every putt held a possibility.

And don't even get me started on bottom-of-the-ninth comebacks. Even the Padres knew how to dazzle us now and again.

But here in the last room, the phantom clock was oppressive. *Tick, tick, tick.* No matter how patiently I invested in all the best behaviors—exercise, a salad instead of a sandwich, sleep—the clock was counting down. I wanted to spend whatever time I had left on the field.

So I chased joy. In Hawaii, Connor, Lucy, and I ate at a decadent restaurant just steps from the sand as the sun gently turned the sky pink, then bright orange, and then peach over the mighty Pacific on Christmas evening. We ordered fancy desserts and made our 2021 predictions. We toasted the year, brimming with gratitude to be sitting in paradise after so many days grinding through cancer and a pandemic. We booked a snorkeling excursion. Dolphins escorted our catamaran out of a secluded bay, one of them winking at me as she crested to take a breath while keeping pace with our vessel.

After more than an hour swimming around and gazing at fish glowing with hues I had never spied up close, I climbed back onto the deck of our boat. I gazed out, watching Connor and Lucy laughing with the new friends they had made in the forty-five minutes we'd spent en route to the snorkeling bay, and decided this: I would crush the short game. If my new game had a lousy clock, I'd take every shot before the buzzer.

And who cared if I occasionally missed? Was anyone even keeping score in the last room? I decided there was minimal reason for reckoning random acts of recklessness in the last room, and I found this alluring.

Besides, I was hardly being reckless. My joy catching more often than not squared on expanding opportunities and adventures for Connor and Lucy, plus my extended family and my dear friends and colleagues at work and all the remarkable progress we were putting in motion through Emerson Collective. My joy catching was more joy spreading, and along the way I wanted more private joy I could call my own.

Sebastien was a skilled surgeon who could remove a tumor as expertly as he could conclude a conversation with a patient. A clean break. Swift. On to what's next, because time—in the form of his intellectual precision, his surgical excellence—was his most precious resource. A clean break enabled him to move to the next patient, save another life. Forward.

So, after the Great Tahoe Debacle of 2020, I drove home fairly confident that he and I would likely never interact in a meaningful way again. The goodbye was far too crushing; he knew he had been careless with me, not to mention whomever it was he was maybe dating. If anyone knew the figurative and literal upsides of a clean cut, it was Sebastien.

I exhibited plenty of intellectual precision too. I knew exactly what was going on, how unbearably crappy it all was. But unlike when the Padres flamed out during one of their occasional playoff runs, there was no next season to pin my hopes—or my heart—on. There was just the last room, and its oppressive clock.

The ridiculous thing was that even after Visser's slumped shoulders in his beautifully tailored suit, I felt perfectly well. I wanted to enjoy life because I had this limited number of days to, well, enjoy.

In any other room, I never would have considered reimagining my friendship with Sebastien. Instead, I would have done the smart and healthy thing—the thing that I had to learn after seven years of postdivorce dating: I would have wished him well and meant it. If we were to stay in touch, it would be appropriate contact and distant, and maybe we'd find our way to a once-a-year coffee to compare notes and cheer on each other's good progress in life.

But I wasn't in any other room. I was in the last room, and I missed him. He continued to reach out and so did I, knowing that seeing him again would result in me settling for a compartmentalized dynamic rather than a true friendship or romance.

I kept going over it and over it. He worked from home, so why wasn't he spending the pandemic in her faraway college town? Was my health a driving factor in his hesitation, and what if I got well? I got why I wasn't staying disciplined with a clean break, but why wasn't he?

Our texts, about the latest *Atlantic* essay where we agreed on much, but not all, of the author's argument, along with the latest back-and-forth about the chaos in politics and *SNL* sketches and all the other big and small, picked up pace. A few weeks after the Great Tahoe Debacle we found our way to walks and hikes, leaving all the awfulness from the prior August unspoken.

I never asked the important questions about his relationship, nor did he ever bring it up. And because we were in the pandemic's prime, the normal rhythm of a friendship—*Join me and my friends for this upcoming concert!*—was off the table. We could make even the existence of our friendship its own compartment. My private corner of the last room.

But I recognized that we were receiving vastly different benefits from this isolating endeavor: Sebastien got to keep me in his life on his own terms, and I got to scrape up the scraps of delight he offered because I had convinced myself this was how to play the short game.

One winter day, we decided to take a drive to Año Nuevo State Park, a beach about an hour and a half southwest, where once a year male elephant seals make their way up onto the sand to take a very long nap while the lady elephant seals camp out a bit farther north to have their pups and nurse and hopefully find time for a nap, too.

But it's the bulls we went to see. These mighty males were snoozing on the beach, having just completed a twelve-thousand-mile swim to their favorite restaurant—a feeding area near the Aleutian Islands. How it is that these elephant seals decided that the fish way off the farthest edge of Alaska are worth the swim is a question for the ages, but I know enough guys who would drive hours for a new kind of doughnut, so I get it.

After snapping up the delicious fare, the bulls turn around and head south and *don't sleep* on the way back. As best as marine biologists can make out, the animals sometimes sneak in a quick catnap in between breaths at the surface, but that's about it. So, with full bellies, they swim thousands of miles south to Año Nuevo, head for the beach, shimmy up the sand, and promptly fall asleep. For days.

Sebastien and I parked near a trail that wound down through wildflowers to a twisty set of stairs that deposited us on the beach. We noticed massive boulders ahead of us, but no critters. Just then a boulder twitched, and we gasped. About fifty yards ahead of us we saw what we thought was a gigantic rock *breathing*. And then, four more. Wait, seven. Each of these mighty elephant seals was slumbering, each like a king on his own sandy throne. We crept closer, but not too close. One flinched, and I mused he must have been having a weird dream.

After a few days of deep sleep, our boys would scoot a mile or so north to meet the ladies, who were nearly done nursing their pups. And once the gentlemen elephant seals made the rendezvous, the annual mating mash-up would commence.

"That one has a George Clooney vibe going," I said, pointing. "I bet he'll get the top pick."

"I don't know," Sebastien countered. "I feel like this one over here is very Denzel and may surprise them all."

Sebastien and I tiptoed around the gorgeous creatures—their snouts are impossible not to love—standing witness to their journey.

As we drove home, Sebastien reached for my hand, and our fingers stayed intertwined as we chatted about everything we had taken in.

When I first illuminated my last room with Paul's virtues, I spent the most time curled up under the reliable heat lamp of excellence. I smiled when I described my top-tier medical team. *How fortunate I am to live so very close to Stanford and UCSF. My God, these physicians are excellence personified.* I understood excellence to be an external standard that resulted from hard work, from discipline, from passion. Excellence is earned.

But the longer I sat near the lantern light of excellence in the last room, I wondered whether Paul was using this word in the way I had come to know it.

Paul was highly educated and must have grown up studying the ancient philosophers. My guess is that he had a copy of Aristotle's *Nicomachean Ethics* tucked into his pack as he trekked along the Via Egnatia to visit his dear ones in Philippi. Aristotle described excellence with a more imaginative flair. Unlike Plato, who put his intellectual weight down on the idea that virtues such as justice and courage and patience could be acquired through rigorous training in the sciences, mathematics, and philosophy, Aristotle reasoned that excellence must be inhabited. In other words, Plato argued excellence came from work, resulting in greater harmony; Aristotle made the case that excellence must be *lived*, purposefully.

The Greek word for excellence is *arete*. And in its original context, *arete* was intimately linked to an individual's fulfillment of purpose, their calling, their essential uniqueness. One scholar described this concept of excellence this way:

> Living with *arete* means having a sense of where one is heading and setting out on that journey to realize what can be accomplished. It implies doing this with competence, precision, and as it must be done. . . .
>
> The Greeks recognized the challenge associated with pursuing excellence and living with purpose. As such, *arete* also implies a sense of bravery. To fulfill one's purpose and to pursue excellence means one will have to overcome obstacles. There will be distractions. There are temptations that will seem like attractive diversions. There will be doubt and insecurities. To remain on the course in the midst of these challenges requires *arete*—the bravery and courage to persevere.

This lamp of excellence that I initially thought spotlighted the prestige of my care started to shift. It began to illuminate how I was inhabiting my own purpose here in the last room. Was excellence something to be earned or an inner commitment to a higher set of values? Was my Western, achievement-oriented view of the world perhaps distorting Paul's intent for the notion of excellence?

Our walks and day trips naturally morphed into long dinners in Sebastien's beautiful San Francisco home. We kept our conversations corralled in all the safe places, a familiar dance we knew well from the months before.

After we cleared the dishes, we'd retire to his living room, with tea, for time on his couch in front of his fireplace, just like before. There, our conversations felt more like a formality, what we both knew was simply a prelude to physical intimacy.

The intimacy always ended the same destructively familiar way: I would gather my things, Sebastien would walk me to my car, and he would ask me to text him when I'd arrived home safely.

I would drive down I-280 and replay it all in my mind, vowing to not let myself fall prey to the temptation of his couch another time. I deserved far more than his couch.

And then I would arrive home, crawl into bed, and savor how it felt to be in his arms. How alive I felt. How desired I felt. How desperately I craved life and desire in the last room. I'd fall asleep knowing it was a terrible trade-off, but this was how playing the short game worked.

This went on for months. And it's why returning to Tahoe together for a weekend of skiing made sense in my distorted frame of mind.

It might be the last weekend with my long hair, and I wanted to enjoy every minute of it. This time, Sebastien booked the Airbnb, a place he said he'd stayed before and so had a discount. I considered what this meant—maybe he'd been there a few weeks earlier with the woman-he-never-spoke-of—and I did my compartmentalized best to say none of that mattered.

We unloaded our gear and settled in, enjoying a long dinner and more couch time before moving to our separate bedrooms. Same show, different location. I had grown accustomed to distortion by now, and I shook off the whispers that reminded me I was disappearing into someone else. A different version of myself who would put up with the ridiculousness of it all.

The next morning we set off for the slopes. After getting on our gear, we sat on a chairlift and took in all that the Sierras offered. A crisp blue sky, fresh snow, and sunny skiing. I'm an average skier, but I love the art of slow improvement. Sebastien was something else. He set out ahead of me and I marveled at his beauty as he flawlessly shifted his weight from side to side and soared down the mountain. I followed as closely as I could just to witness such grace and artistry.

On a chairlift a while later, I told him what I was seeing. "You're a beautiful skier, Sebastien," I said. "Truly. You are beauty in motion."

"Oh, thanks," he said. "You know, with a lesson or two you could for sure become more confident. You have the basics, you just need a little help with technique to trust the skis."

"Mm-hmm," I replied, knowing this was likely the last time I would ever ski. I was a week away from resuming chemo and losing my hair, and the idea that I would find some new chapter in this last room to take up intermediate skiing lessons seemed farcical.

So, instead, I savored the day. Savored Sebastien's skiing prowess and the magnificence of the Sierras and how it felt to be skiing among the living.

We went back to the house, dusted off the snow, and settled into a long dinner. We curled up to watch a movie, but I barely remember any of it. Instead, knowing how the night would unfold, I began my mental self-talk about how the short game is played. Live for the moment, take what you can get, which isn't much.

The dance continued in my bedroom. Fully intimate, but eerily compartmentalized.

In the morning, I woke up alone, vaguely aware that I could hear Sebastien upstairs packing up the food for the drive home. I could still smell his scent in my bed. He likely left me alone in the middle of the night. The sunlight brought clarity to the distortion I'd chosen to set aside in the prior evening's darkness: I was confusing Sebastien's physical affection for evidence that he thought I might live longer. Every kiss, every couch dance, every time we crossed every kind of line, I banked it all as Sebastien conveying to me this: *You are healthy. You are an attractive, fully alive woman. You aren't going anywhere because I am here with you in this most intimate way.*

I stared at the ceiling, eyes brimming with tears. Of course, Sebastien never once had said these words to me, so what was I doing conflating my hopes and his libido? My complicity unleashed chaos in my exhausted brain and confused heart.

We barely spoke of any of it on the drive home, but in my madness, I muttered a half apology when we arrived at his house. "I probably put you in a complicated position, and I'm sorry about that," I said.

"Oh, it's fine," he said. "I get it. It's all complicated. And listen, make sure you tell me how things go for you this week."

On chemo, I'd never thrown up, but in that moment all I wanted to do was vomit in Sebastien's kitchen as we said our goodbyes.

Weeks later, I recounted the whole pathetic tale to a friend also named Amy. Amy holds a special place in my life. Among her other attributes, she's always been the most unfiltered. This can be thrilling or terrifying, depending on the day.

I was in Santa Barbara visiting friends, enjoying feeling semi-normal after a round of chemo. I called Amy while walking on the beach and related Tahoe 2.0. She listened carefully, mirroring back to me what she thought I had said. She replayed it all with an uncanny specificity, and I felt both heard and loved. After recapping, she asked me if she'd gotten it right.

"Yes, you got it. I know. It's so terrible!" I said.

"Okay," Amy said. "I guess I have only one question."

"Go for it," I said.

"My question is this: When, exactly, did you start hating yourself so much? I mean, did it happen years ago and I missed it? Or is this relatively new? This is the only thing I really need to ask."

I stopped on the sand and looked out on the crashing waves. "What are you talking about? The only reason I'm in this mess is because I have cancer and anyone would be in this Sebastien pretzel," I said.

"Bullshit," she said. "I don't give a fuck about the cancer. Who cares that you have cancer. You've decided you're okay being treated this way, which means that somewhere along the way you must have decided you're not worth much. Which means that today you hate yourself. And I'm just wondering, was this always the case or is it kind of new?"

Well, shit.

I spent the rest of that afternoon walking around Westmont, my college campus, which slopes up and down a hill overlooking Santa Barbara. I needed the exercise before my five-hour drive home and time to clear my head. So, I parked in the lower campus and maneuvered to the top, pausing along the way to stand outside the building where my classes had expanded my intellect and my imagination.

I lingered in the courtyard of the dorm where I'd spent a year living with Ashley and Tiffany, two dear friends who had reentered my story since learning of my diagnosis. I kept walking and eventually took a seat outside of a lecture hall where I'd fallen in love with studying history and where a professor named Shirley challenged all of her young undergraduates to wrestle with the question: "What is the good life?" It's the question that framed Plato's argument linking excellence with work and Aristotle's counterargument concluding that excellence comes from within if we stay tethered to our true selves. Paul's answer was to list the virtues now lighting my last room.

Soon after my time in Santa Barbara, I reached out to Shirley, who was broadly in the loop about my diagnosis. It's important to know that Shirley holds two PhDs (history and philosophy) and is the clearest thinker I know. We set a time to chat, and after catching her up on my progress, setbacks, progress, and setbacks, I teed up my question. "Okay, well, I suppose I need to start out by saying I've stopped flossing," I said. "I mean, I still brush my teeth and care for my gums, but I've decided I can drop some things, because I'm in the last room."

Shirley got it immediately.

"Also, I'm taking my kids on extravagant trips. Just a few weeks ago, Lucy and I spontaneously flew off to New York City and we made the theme of our time 'fancy,' which means every time we could upgrade—a flight, theater tickets, a dress we saw in a window—we would say yes. It was all glorious, and slightly crazy. I'm tipping with all kinds of abandon these days, too. I do this knowing that very soon I'll be paying college tuition, so these are semireckless financial decisions, but if I'm gone, the kids will be taken care of. It's a bizarre rationalization, but I think most people would understand it.

"And, well, I have this dear friend, Sebastien," I said. I described how he occupied a precious place in my life—he had saved it a few times now—and how impossible it would be for me to let him drift away.

"But it's more than that," I said. "I'm now intertwined in a friendship where the lines are constantly crossed, and it's just not how I normally operate. But can't we agree that it's entirely okay to play the short game in the long-game world? This is my question for you. I thought you might have a thought."

"You sound really stressed," she said. "What I mean is, stress that's more than cancer."

"Yes," I said. "I think that's right. Or maybe not. Maybe this is just how anyone sounds in the last room. So, anyhow, what do you think about this notion of playing the short game? It makes sense, right?"

Shirley was quiet and then said this, "Well, you're actually asking one of the biggest questions of all. There's so much at work here with what you're raising. I need a few days to think about this. Let's plan to talk a week from today."

I agreed, marveling that she would take such care with what I was asking. I knew what I was doing: I was hoping Shirley could ease my anxiety and assure me that anyone would take advantage of last-room hall passes the way I was.

The following week, Shirley called me back, just as she'd promised. We got right into it.

"So, let me ask you this," she began. "Are you still making your bed?"

"Umm. Yes," I replied.

"Paying your bills? Bringing your best to career?"

"Yes, and yes," I said. "In some ways I've never been more on top of things."

"And these trips you're taking with the kids. They've loved them too?"

"Yes," I said. "I mean, it's a little unusual for us, but we're loving these adventures."

She took a deep breath. "Okay," she said. "I'd like to suggest something about this last room. This extraordinary room that is likely the end of your life. This place where you know you reside, and where most days you feel so physically well even knowing that your long-term prospects are so dire.

"I want to suggest that this is holy ground, this last room. This space you're occupying is hallowed, and I think you know this. Few people get to be in this room, waking up every day feeling well and knowing that they are there.

"But you do. And I want to suggest that the invitation of the room is to become *more of who you are.* These short-game decisions, as you call them, are not all the same. When you tip extra, it's a deeper extension of who you've always been. When you take Connor and Lucy to Hawaii, it's true to the kind of experiences you've always wanted for them. You've described this fellowship portfolio you've built at Emerson, and this is in keeping with the imagination you've always brought to your career. These are decisions that might have more urgency, might have more intensity, but they are in deep alignment with who you are."

I listened carefully knowing there was more to come.

"But when you discuss this friendship with Sebastien, I hear something else. I hear you giving yourself permission to become someone you are not. Would you have stayed in this kind of blurry space if you weren't in the last room?"

"No," I confessed. "But I simply don't have a choice. It's the last room, and it's the only intimacy I have. And, well, I love him."

"I can hear that in your voice," she said. "And that makes it all so tender, and so heartbreaking. But I want to suggest something to you, and it might not be easy to hear. I think you've navigated three distinct betrayals in your life, which is more than really anyone should ever bear. You've moved through Don's betrayal and the death of your marriage. And then you've been living through the betrayal of your body, when a group of cells decided to deviate from a healthy path and instead create a disease. But the third betrayal is by far the most devastating. It's the *betrayal of yourself* within this complicated friendship with Sebastien.

"Amy, this last room is calling you to become, well, more Amy. Your true self, the person you were born to be. You're moving farther up and farther into this last room, and you're discovering wonders you've never seen before. I can hear it in your voice. It's a marvel. But your voice cracks when you talk about your heart and how you continue to settle for an unrequited love.

"From how you've described it, Sebastien isn't a villain in this story. He's been entirely consistent with you. And he's provided you with such generous medical thought partnership and connections. He's heroic, in all kinds of ways. But what he's offered you is less than what you would have accepted before the last room. You're the one who decided this heartbreaking compromise was worth, as you say, the short game.

"Here is the reality of the last room—it's the place where the fruits of the long game are in clearest abundance. Seize them. Savor them. And summon the courage to tap into the truest story of all—yours."

Sebastien read a lung scan better than anyone on my medical team. But in this conversation, Shirley gave a read of my heart that was as compassionate as it was revelatory.

"Oh, and on the flossing," she added. "That's kind of on you and your gums. I have no idea if that's true to who you are or not. Maybe ask your dentist."

Lately, I've been thinking about those glorious elephant seals and their amazing annual journey. These sleeping and swimming giants—some weigh in at more than four thousand pounds—are all the more astounding when you consider that just a hundred years ago the mighty elephant seal was nearly extinct. By some estimates, fewer than a hundred elephant seals survived the decades of rampant hunting for their oil-rich blubber.

With their numbers dwindled to just a few dozen, elephant seals as a species were in their own last room. But then wise law-makers in 1922 created protections and gave the seals a chance to live fully and without fear of being wiped out.

These creatures had only one job: Be their most excellent elephant seal selves and set off on that twelve-thousand-mile swim the way their ancestors did. They came back because decade after decade they stayed true to the core of their calling, as whacky as it might be.

They didn't stray. Instead, every year, they swam from the tip of Baja California all the way up to a small set of islands in the Gulf of Alaska to find just the right feeding spot. Along the way, they grunted and clicked in some marvelous elephant seal secret language and encouraged each other, reminding each other they were born for this journey, that they are among a small group of species who go so far to reach their destination. They probably also shared tales of the most luxurious sandy beach along Northern California's coastline, where sleep will come in a way that feels like paradise—why not?

In my head, the conversation goes like this:

"It's too far! There are only a few of us left! Maybe let's go to Cabo and find Mexican food instead."

"Keep going, swim, swim more. Find that special cove made just for you. Because there in that cove will be nourishment and fuel for the swim home. Loop back, keep swimming.

"Lady elephant seals, you have pups to birth. Keep swimming.

"Manly elephant seals, you have a nap to take. Keep swimming.

"You were created exactly for this twelve-thousand-mile swim. Aristotle called this kind of swim *arete*, and there will be days when you'll be exhausted. Be brave. Trust this swim.

"Be true to who you are. You are part of something so very excellent."

Today elephant seals are still a protected species, but their numbers have rebounded, magnificently. There are at least two hundred thousand swimming twelve thousand miles round trip each year, bravely dreaming of a sandy beach on which to lay their adorable elephant seal heads.

I'd like to say that after Shirley's careful read of my heart scan that I surgically resected Sebastien's couch from my life, but I'll admit it took far longer than it should have. The shift to a purely platonic friendship took an extraordinary amount of time, and I surrounded that journey with an abundance of compassion and grace for my wounded and very open heart.

Unlike elephant seals, who have no self-consciousness about their strenuous annual swim, I had honest choices to confront as

I stumbled between grasping for short-term thrills and reclaiming my long-term self, my long-term dignity.

The great gift and burden of the last room slowly revealed itself. If my job after Don's betrayal was to step into a season of recovery and rebuilding, the invitation before me now was to embrace a deeper reckoning of my own worth.

The last room is often terrifying and exhausting. As the drama continued to unfold, Sebastien offered an enchanting bivouac—an intermission between the hard scenes playing out on the stage of my life when I could wander out to the lobby and feel beautiful and adored rather than broken and sick. I cherished those intermissions and went back time and time again.

And yet when the lights dimmed and the story onstage resumed, as it always did, the intermissions became brutal reminders that whatever was happening out in the lobby—Sebastien's short-game invitation—was not my story at all.

The more I allowed myself to dwell ever more deeply in an asymmetric relationship, the more comfortable I became with distortion. I told myself the last room was itself distorted, so any self-distortion was eerily consistent, and therefore the cosmic math worked, maybe.

But there was no math in motion. Only deviations.

The word *integrity* comes from the Latin adjective *integer*, meaning "whole" or "complete." It is defined as "an undivided or unbroken completeness." In English, an integer is a whole number; it cannot be divided.

Sebastien was and is beautiful and our friendship was never one thing. He entered my story just at the right time. He championed my care, drew close to the most intricate details, provided context and clarity for the pages of the playbook that were most confusing. He opened doors to ever more expertise and held me close when I whispered to him late at night that I was so very frightened. And so very exhausted.

He was consistent with me throughout. What he offered—romantically—was at times sweet, but never substantial. Never whole.

Because I set aside my own integrity, I deviated from the magic of the last room: the opportunity to become closer to my true self, even when this required sacrificing a short-term delight in favor of a long-term, and far more beautiful, investment.

The lamp of excellence in the last room eventually became a mirror. I found my way to it—stumbled, really—and looked at my reflection. I saw myself. My true self. The one God created me to be. I was never more alive.

I gazed at the person I was becoming, and for the first time since my diagnosis I didn't hear the clock ticking.

If Anything Is Praiseworthy

Ten cycles of FOLFIRI worked, mostly. Throughout the spring and summer of 2021, I withstood all the chemo rounds with optimism and endurance: chemo had reliably worked for me, which fueled my persistence in tolerating a range of annoying side effects. The more patients I came to know, the more I understood how fortunate I was to describe chemo as something I was "tolerating." Many others used the word *suffering.* Every time I concluded a round, rather than feeling relieved, as they described, I found that gratitude held hands with sorrow; the paradoxical mindsets were now coiled together like fraternal twins rather than distant cousins.

The treatment resulted in nearly all the lung itty-bitties getting demoted to teeny-tinies, minus two stubborn mets that appeared to outsmart the chemo. After careful consultation with Dr. Ko, we decided to welcome a new medical pro into the story: a radiation oncologist named Dr. Feng, whom I promptly nicknamed Princess Leia.

The longer I bounced among chemo and surgery and living, the more I began to wonder about radiation for my itty-bitties. My story was lengthening from a tightly plotted tale to a saga, and—having raised Connor and Lucy to appreciate the full canon of *Star Wars* adventures—I reasoned that every memorable saga at some point would have some laser beams in play.

When we had a video consult, Leia brought her A game. "You're an ideal candidate," she declared after a few minutes of getting to know me and my images. "We can work out a beautiful treatment schedule for you in the coming weeks."

I loved that she referred to her laser beams as "beautiful." Or at least the treatment schedule. In any case, Princess Leia used this word the way that I did, and I was certain we'd become allies. Maybe even friends. So far, zero of my doctors ever suggested we have lunch sometime, but now my hopes were pinned on Princess Leia. I mentioned that I was now calling my slightly shortened colon a semicolon, and she flashed me a fabulous smile.

"Oh, I *love* that," she said. "That's a new one."

"I know!" I responded. "Don't you think we ought to figure out merch or something for those of us whose semicolons are doing all the work of their colon predecessors?"

"Absolutely," she said. We so got each other.

We never met in real life.

Instead, I showed up to my first radiation appointment at UCSF and was escorted to a room I can only describe as the command center of a starship. A tricked-out space featuring a dazzling console bejeweled with an array of monitors and blinking lights, the room was dimly illuminated from above by recessed blue bulbs. Leia was nowhere to be found.

Two lieutenants approached me—efficient nurses, each with a determined stride.

"Wow, it's like we're flying through outer space in here," I said.

"Keep walking, please. Through this door. BUT DO NOT TOUCH IT," the lieutenant warned. "It will open on its own."

I then stepped into a larger hull, but instead of a series of digital consoles, the interior room featured a massive cylindrical structure with a small plank where I was instructed to lie flat. I was familiar with scanners, but this was far more massive. More like a submarine than a narrow tube.

I did as I was instructed, vaguely aware that the next step would involve some manner of snorkel gear. Princess Leia had mentioned that radiation wasn't all that physically hard, but it did involve wearing a device akin to a VR headset coupled with a snorkel mouthpiece and nose clips. My job was this: relax, breathe through my mouth, keep my eyes focused on the little blue line visible in the eyewear contraption thing, and when told to "HOLD," hold my breath for as long as the blue line appeared on my tiny screen.

As soon as I got settled, I realized how much I dearly loved breathing through my nose. I tried to concentrate on how marvelous it had been to snorkel with Connor and Lucy just months before in Hawaii and how I was able to gracefully deal with being a mouth breather then. But instead of tropical fish, all I had to see was an oppressive blue line that never seemed to end—

HOLD.

I inhaled, held my breath, and kept my eyes fixed on the blue line to keep my inhale as steady as possible. Instead of visualizing fish, I pivoted to the dazzling wonder of how Princess Leia's laser beams were—in that moment—blasting the itty-bitties to bits.

OK, RELAX.

Deep mouth breaths—

HOLD.

Inhale, focus, blue line. Focus: *Did Princess Leia go to target-shooting practice when she was a girl? Or did her dad teach her on the weekends the way my dad taught me how to keep score at baseball games? This blue line will never end.*

OK, RELAX.

The lieutenants kept at it for ten blue-line sessions. The massive door slowly opened, and the two entered to release me from the snorkel gear of oppression.

"That's it?" I asked.

"Yes, that's it," they said.

"Okay, do I go meet with Dr. Feng now?"

"Nope. You're free to go. See you tomorrow."

Maybe Princess Leia was monitoring all of this from her own starship in a solar system down the hall? Or was this a pandemic thing?

I walked through the door that I was not allowed to touch, down to the exit, and then across the courtyard to my car. I looked around and wondered who else searching for their car had just had lasers beamed into them. Something remarkable had just happened inside my precious lung tissue—a microscopic explosion and I didn't feel anything.

I repeated that whole journey another five times—three sessions each for the two itty-bitties—and got chummy enough with Leia's lieutenants to get them to loosen up a bit while we walked down the hallway and approach the door that must not be touched.

"This is all so extraordinary," I said. "How many patients do you, um, radiate on any given day?"

"Oh, it varies," a lieutenant said. "But usually at least ten or so."

"Ahh. Well, it's so much easier than surgery. But that nose-pincher thing is a drag."

"Yeah, we hear that a lot," the lieutenant said. "You handle it all really well, though. Most times, you hold your breath about seventy-five seconds, and that's terrific. We have some patients who can only go about ten seconds before having to exhale."

"Wow," I said, feeling proud. "Huh. Yeah, well, you know I try to stay active even with all of the chemo and the rest. Some think I'm the healthiest stage IV cancer lady they've ever met..."

"Mm-hmm," the lieutenant said, fussing with the snorkel gear. "Then again nearly all of our patients are in their seventies, so I guess it's not fair to compare."

My pride evaporated. I scrolled through my Instagram feed and saw my friends—same age as me—using their free time to vacation with their healthy and intact families or to play as much tennis as they pleased. I wondered for what seemed like the millionth time: *How did I end up in this mess?* I was still silently asking this unanswerable question, even two and a half years after my diagnosis.

Meanwhile, the question most asked of me by others remained: How are the kids doing?

I adored when people asked, despite the frequency. Like Leia's laser beams, the question got to the heart of all this mess. How were Connor and Lucy living with the specter of losing their mom? The question revealed that the inquirer understood the true project at hand: if I had to sashay off my stage early, Connor and Lucy would be the ones who would be called to hold the heaviest burden of grief.

Eventually, as they moved through the long years of their adulthood, some of their memories of me would fade. And yet my loss would be a wound they would work their entire lives to heal. And I wouldn't be with them to help them heal it.

You've raised them well. Kids are so resilient. They will be fine.

These are well-intentioned reassurances, but all I could think was, *Yes, yes, and no.*

So, normally, when asked, I would say the kids were in great shape. Because, for the most part, they were. Despite the pandemic, they found their friend groups and pursued their passions and were getting ready to go off to college.

But sometimes friends would ask how Lucy and Connor were faring in a way that indicated they wanted to draw closer to the most forbidding corner of the last room. The place where fear was most present and persistent. They probed, carefully and gently, trying to join me there. To acknowledge that this corner—this notion of leaving my children too early—was impossible, unbearable.

It was during those tear-drenched chats when I would inevitably mention how horrible it was that I had never taken Connor and Lucy to Italy.

When I lived in Washington, DC, in my late twenties, and Don was in Seattle, our first date had happened in San Francisco when I'd traveled there for work. I was initially stunned when he'd suggested having dinner there when he didn't live anywhere near San Francisco. I'd begged off a bit, assuming I was misreading a signal or two.

"Oh, I don't know," I'd written. "Flying all the way from Seattle to San Francisco for dinner seems like quite a lift, and I'm sure you've got so much going on."

His response was quintessential Don. "I don't know what you had in mind. . . . I was just hoping we could have dinner."

Well played.

Our dinner was a spectacular one, and it spilled into a day of wine tasting in Napa the day after. The drive back to San Francisco to catch our flights was full of big talk about the next chance we might have for a hello. And within days, I was searching for flights so I could meet him in Tuscany a few weeks later—he'd made plans months earlier to celebrate his fortieth birthday cycling with a friend through Italy's rolling hills and suggested I pop over for the final weekend when the cycling would be concluded. I had just enough miles stashed away to make it work.

We spent part of the weekend in Siena, gazing at frescoes, walking on cobblestone streets, and sitting in the city's famed center square, taking in Italy's splendor. We spent the weekend falling in love, surrounded by ancient splendor.

I had been to Italy other times—I was lucky to study abroad there and had experienced just enough Italian vacations to know my way around the central attractions, as well as the easy-to-miss churches that never leave your soul. I was by no means an Italy expert, but it was where my imagination grew exponentially as a student, and where my heart became besotted with another's.

I wanted to walk along Italy's ancient cobblestones with Connor and Lucy. I wanted to take them to a place where beauty has a stubborn streak—maybe glimpse them embracing the awe.

My late-night Italy plotting became a proxy for all the magnificence I wished Lucy and Connor would experience throughout their lives without a mom to call or text or put an arm around. With the virus's variants spiking and the pandemic barely subsiding, and with the constant uncertainty about what the next scan might hold—not to mention the kids being on different academic calendars—an Italian getaway grew ever more elusive.

But a small window of opportunity emerged. Princess Leia's beautiful treatment plan included a fourteen-day pause the last two weeks of December.

"How will I be feeling then?" I asked her on one of our video chats.

"Probably fine," she said. "Maybe a little sluggish, but that's likely it."

I knew sluggish. I knew how to crush sluggish. I knew how to take sluggish on the road.

Christmas in Rome and then a few days in Florence? I put our plan in motion, letting both kids know that this year instead of a tree and presents and our church's Christmas Eve service, we were going to have the pope and St. Peter's Square and not a small amount of pizza. I couldn't care less about the Omicron variant swirling about.

One of my favorite movies is *Chariots of Fire*. It's a true tale of two runners from the United Kingdom in 1924—Eric Liddell, a devout Christian from Scotland, and Harold Abrahams, an English Jew. Both gifted runners, Eric and Harold each held a deep spiritual devotion that accelerated their ambition and their pace on the track. Harold battled toxic anti-Semitism; Eric grappled with his own sense of calling, a pull between his running and his desire to share his faith in China.

In the film, as Eric accumulates wins and accolades, his sister confronts him on a steep Scottish hillside, terrified that his running is clouding his sense of judgment about the path she believes God has prepared for him. On that jagged mountain, Eric says this to his worried sister:

> I believe that God made me for a purpose. For China. But He also made me fast, and when I run, I feel His pleasure. To give it up would be to hold Him in contempt . . . to win is to honor Him.

As my last room grew ever brighter, illuminated by Paul's virtues—truth, nobility, a trail toward what's right, what's pure, what's lovely and also excellent—I came to see new contours of beauty surrounding my story and even the room itself. Beauty came in the form of my deeper understanding of excellence—I began to see, or rather appreciate, souls moving closer to their purpose, the place where, as writer Frederick Buechner famously said, "your deep gladness meets the world's deep need."

In those places, God's pleasure becomes beauty for us all to behold. It's a holy place, one worthy of praise.

Two years to the day since my abdominal surgery, Connor, Lucy, and I waited, with our suitcases packed, passports renewed, and COVID tests sorted out for our flight to Rome. As our Uber pulled up to the house, Connor dashed upstairs to his room to fetch his trumpet.

"You're bringing your trumpet?" I asked impatiently, wondering how we'd manage so many bags.

"Mom, I'll need to practice while we're away. Plus, you know, it's always good to keep a trumpet close."

I was skeptical but knew I didn't have a vote in the matter. The kids had become expert packers at a young age when they'd begun flying solo to see Don years before. Connor would manage his bags and didn't need me second-guessing his decisions.

I had only experienced Rome in the summer; we landed on the winter solstice, but Rome kept the lights on for us—twinkle lights, to be precise. Antiquated streets were draped with canopies of tiny bulbs, welcoming us at nearly every corner.

We walked the Vatican gardens, climbed to the top of St. Peter's in time to gaze out at a pastel sunset, paid our respects to the Pantheon, stared up for as long as our necks would allow in the Sistine Chapel, dodged the city's tiny cars, listened to Rick Steves guide us through the Colosseum and the Forum, marveled at Bernini's sculptures, and joined thousands of other souls on Christmas morning to hear the pope's message. *Buon natale*, we said to our taxi drivers, waiters, and fellow marvelers.

The day after Christmas we boarded a train bound for Florence. As we made our way north, I read through some Florence guidebooks I'd brought along and spotted a small sentence tucked into the overviews of museums and historic sites: "Several scholars agree that, because of the plague, by 1352 the population of Florence had dropped to less than half of what it had been at the start of 1348."

Half. Half of a city's population perished from a terrible disease over the course of four years. I glanced around the train, adjusting the mask on my face to fit a bit more snugly. I wondered how many people in our car had lost loved ones to COVID, especially during those early and horrific weeks when the world wept for Lombardy. The Omicron variant was growing stronger. We were cautioned that Florence was adopting new protocols, including museum and church closures. Staring out at the night's sky through the train window, I realized we'd likely not get to see Michelangelo's *David* in the Accademia Gallery the way I had planned.

Michelangelo was born very near Florence in 1475, so he must have grown up hearing tales of the plague and how his ancestors had survived. Also how their children had persevered and how the next generation began to rebuild. Did those previous generations somehow equip Michelangelo and his contemporaries with a deeper vision to reimagine, to renew?

Would Connor and Lucy someday tell their own children about the pandemic? How they Zoomed and kept their cameras off and unmuted like champs and even played the occasional ukulele during class? Would their children's kiddos hear these tales and discover an inner stirring to birth a new era of beauty?

Our Florentine days were spent mostly outside. Bundled up in our coats and scarves, we walked along the Arno, studied the

Duomo's golden doors, and wondered why more US cities didn't take a page out of Florence's playbook and close core streets to cars, allowing pedestrians to roam freely.

One midday, just four blocks from our Airbnb apartment, we came upon three street musicians in the Piazza del Repubblica playing the kind of jazz riffs I had come to know well from all of Connor's gigs and school concerts. Live music was a rarity during pandemic spikes, so we paused to savor their spirited sounds. As we listened, I caught a glimmer in Connor's eyes above his mask, knowing we were thinking the same thing.

"How about you go get your trumpet and see if you can join in?" I asked.

He was off, dashing down the cobblestones. Minutes later, Connor returned and cautiously approached the trio, trumpet in hand, and politely asked to join in.

One of the musicians had enough English to say, "Why not?"

What followed next was thirty minutes of jazz improvs and trumpet riffs, a mash-up of melodies that found a delightful harmony. Three older Italians and one young American creating something new on an ancient square.

Lucy and I smiled and then glanced around, noticing a small crowd forming. Italian kiddos started to dance, their parents clapped, and more joined in. As COVID's terrible variant crept all around us, a crowd swirled with a more powerful force multiplier: joy.

As I watched the laughing and dancing, I witnessed a shift. This moment of music on the Piazza del Repubblica would carry a new story for me and for my fellow Italian revelers. I made eye contact with enough of them to know they would carry with them a tale about an impromptu burst of song on a winter's day. On a day when we were all masked up, when the museums began to shutter again, and when we were all careful to space out just so. On this ominous day of Omicron, the story we'd tell that night would be about an unlikely foursome and their spontaneous high notes rather than about case numbers and hospitalizations.

Perhaps those are the kinds of stories Michelangelo heard growing up in Florence. Stories of pandemic survivors creating beauty amid sorrow, stories of light overcoming darkness. Maybe the narrative from that oral history inspired one generation after another to spur an era that would change everything. A reimagination. A renaissance.

New is made possible by paying close attention to our calling. Investing in our craft—whether it's firing laser beams with perfect precision or hitting a high note on a trumpet—is the pursuit of sheer delight. Surely, this is what Paul meant by concluding his list of virtues with the word *praiseworthy*.

Maybe Paul was speaking of the truth I discovered on that Italian square—pack your instrument. Practice, be ready, bring your full self, which is to say your heart, to these days. Peaceful days and pandemic days. Pack your instrument. A miracle may already be in motion.

Create something new from what's most familiar—the gift you were born to share with others. When you share this gift, it may very well be worthy of praise. A new story will be told.

THINK ABOUT SUCH THINGS

My story ends with a beginning.

Lung mets reappeared on my February 2022 scan, but they were small. Dr. Ko declared them to be "indolent," a fancy word for lazy. I continued to feel well, and it was becoming increasingly clear that my cancer story had graduated from a straightforward playbook—with obvious decisions and marching orders—to a far more nuanced set of judgment calls.

"Should I resume chemo?" I would ask Ko and Colocci.

They would answer in similar fashion.

"There's no rush here," Ko would say. "But sometime this year you'll want to start treatment again. How would you like your year to go?"

"There's no one right answer here," Colocci would say. "It's really your decision."

I would relay this lack of clarity to my friends and family, most of whom had the natural impulse to call it all madness.

"That's ridiculous!" they would say. "You shouldn't have to make these hard decisions by yourself!"

They weren't wrong. But I knew that my story no longer held obvious direction signs, and despite my brilliant medical team's discernment and candor, I was now the best person to sort out my dual goals: quality and quantity of days.

The year 2022 was, for the most part, a delight. I held off on more chemotherapy, content knowing that my lung itty-bitties were, for now, being quite lazy—like teenagers curled up on the couch in a world where if they didn't throw away their empty pizza boxes piling up in the kitchen, someone else likely would. And I woke up nearly every day feeling not just well but healthy. Long hikes resumed, travel resumed, Connor thrived in college, and Lucy and I discovered what fun it was to create a little twosome as she tackled her academically arduous junior year and spent her evenings in the dance studio.

But the reckoning would come—there was never a doubt about that. And by early fall, the mets had grown just enough that we all agreed it was time to hit it again, this time with Foxy.

After a total of thirty-four rounds of varying types of chemo, my March 2023 scan revealed that my once-indolent lung mets all were a little bigger. Sebastien read the scan carefully for me and said in a kind but matter-of-fact voice that one met was now technically a mass. He didn't notice that I wiped away tears hearing that new word enter our lexicon.

The day I'd seen Visser's shoulders slumped within that beautiful suit of his back in 2021, I'd understood that the story of my colon cancer was now actually the story of my lung. And I'd understood that my journey was now about adding time, as much time as I could receive. But I'd also known that no one can withstand an unlimited number of chemo rounds. I had completed thirty-four. There would be no more rounds for me. My cancer cells had found a way to outsmart the breathtakingly complex chemical compounds that had kept me alive for nearly four years.

This part of my story had reached a conclusion. And like all good stories, a new chapter emerged.

In the earlier rooms of my life, facing hard facts was never easy, but I had hope about future rooms to help lessen the sting. A hard turn in my career could be outlasted, or contextualized, as a stepping stone to the next challenge. A breakup? It would wound, yes, but I could find a way to pivot the conclusion into a beginning and a door to another chamber.

But in the last room, the facts—the white spots on my scans that I could see with my own eyes—were like paintings on the walls, showing me the truth of my life.

The problem, of course, with hard facts in the last room is that there is no way to transform the brutal truths into something else. There is only sitting with them. There is only absorbing them.

If the last room calls us to anything, it's the courage to grapple, to face it all. The courage to say, "Yes, there it is, and it's awful." This seeing—this knowing—requires far more bravery than our first and well-intentioned instincts lend. Those adorable instincts that insist that it can't be as bad as we might think.

These minimizing instincts arrive first mainly because they are so generously invitational for others to find a way to draw close. Close friends and family say, "Come here—let's share best-case scenarios. Let's talk about hopeful possibilities, and maybe that will make us all feel comforted." It's a well-intended table, one with plenty of seats for loving souls who bring optimism, which is to say, tales of the bright side.

But the grappling table is a lonelier place. It's quiet at this table. Often, there's not much to say. And that's what makes this table the holiest of all: the grappling is actually a hushed coming alongside. It is holding a hand while absorbing the enormity of it all.

One of my last-room heroes—Dietrich Bonhoeffer—wrote hundreds of letters to his beloveds while he lived his last-room days during World War II in a German prison. He was incarcerated for being a part of the resistance, part of a group that ultimately devised a plan to assassinate Hitler. Dietrich was a Lutheran pastor who saw his own faith community succumb to abhorrent Nazi policies, choosing personal and community safety over the scriptural commands to stand for justice and for the oppressed.

For Dietrich, his scans came in the form of ominous signs that his Nazi captors meant to move him and his fellow resisters to more oppressive quarters and eventually to the gallows. The signals were unmistakable.

In a letter to his friend Eberhard Bethge during Christmastime in 1943, Dietrich wrote this:

> The past few weeks have been more difficult emotionally than all of what preceded them. But there is nothing more that can be done about it, only that it is more difficult to resign oneself to something one believes could have been prevented than to what is unavoidable. But once the facts are settled, one way or the other, one must then come to terms with them. . . .
>
> Once everything has been tried and failed, then it is much easier to bear. It's true that not everything that happens is simply "God's will." But in the end nothing happens "apart from God's will" (Matthew 10:29), that is, in every event, even the most ungodly, there is a way through to God.

In Dietrich's letter I found a last-room soulmate. He was sorting out the facts, and the facts were awful. But his letter reveals something more: the notion that God, or something bigger than us, faces the facts alongside us. Ultimately, Dietrich wrestles with the hardest problem of all—how can an onslaught of horror happen in a life aimed at goodness?

In addition to the many wise observations my friend Shirley has given me, she once said something that helps me wrestle with the paradox Dietrich raises—this duality that God never designed the mets in my lung (or Nazis, for that matter) and yet, somehow, all of this insanity still exists within a higher purpose.

Shirley said, "Nothing is wasted in God's economy."

She said this to me at a time when I didn't have the imagination to appreciate its implications, and when the problem of evil resided in abstract discussions. But within cancer, within scans, within my last room, her words helped link all of the standalone lamps of Paul's virtues into a constellation of luminescence to help me find my way.

A constellation creates shapes—stories—a more profound narrative that hints at a holy economy taking shape. This, as Dietrich said, is the way through to God. Believing in something that's bigger than us protects us from what some philosophers call the human condition: that we are alone in the world.

I have a friend named Sri, a physician who dedicates part of his year to training other physicians in some of the world's most resource-deprived places as a way to strengthen local health systems. He once said this: "My job as a doctor is to ensure that my patients die of old age." A notion that might feel simple, and yet the more time I spent thinking about how he described his life's calling, the more I came to understand the most important lesson of the last room.

Things that are true, noble, right, pure, lovely, admirable, and excellent and praiseworthy are guides, lights for us all.

But they are more than that. They can be transformed into imaginative new doors, passageways, exits for those dwelling in the last room who have no business being there.

A five-year-old girl in Sierra Leone who is malnourished should never be in the last room. She does not belong there.

A young man growing up on the South Side of Chicago—a neighborhood riddled with senseless gun violence—might be in the last room. He shouldn't be there, either.

A young family living in Ukraine who falls asleep at night to the sounds of shelling and has dreams clouded by terror. They are in the last room, and they shouldn't be.

A forty-eight-year-old single mom of two magnificent teenagers shouldn't be in the last room, either.

I've called Paul's virtues lights in that they illuminate the path for all of us who might have the heart to discover the exits for those in the last room too soon. Like doctors, who are trained to find those passageways, each of us can commit to this grander invitation to healing, no matter our vocation.

Through our time, our votes, our financial gifts, our voices, and our listening, we can ignite goodness. We can reach out, hold the hand of a beloved in a last room, and point toward that passageway to more years, more life. We can expand the plot of an individual's story; we can create a far more interdependent set of stories that link us all.

In the days following the distressing scan, I enrolled in a clinical trial, a new approach using immunotherapy rather than chemotherapy. The trial holds good promise, but these are early days and the last room has become ever more fragile.

Join me, for a moment, here. As I receive this new treatment, I look up at the small pouch of immunotherapy that drips into my veins and marvel at the possibility these drugs might provide me more life.

But I also see something—or, rather, someone—else.

I see a mom raising two teenagers in 2034. She's wonderful, this mom. She has endured so much—she lost her spouse, the love of her life. But she found her footing, and she discovered the middle school years with her kids were hilarious because those fourteen- and twelve-year-old creatures knew how to laugh at the world's best jokes.

She's carried sorrow, but she's reached for joy as often as she could. She risked. She kept her heart open.

She listened as her kids told her stories, and she learned to ask questions in a way that elicited more nuance from them. She went to back-to-school nights by herself and did her best, sprinting from one room to another. She discovered teachers who loved her kids, and she gave thanks for them.

She learned how to forgive, and it took a long time.

She advanced goodness in her career and set powerful momentum in motion. She cheered on her colleagues and looked for ways to give credit away.

She fell in love again.

And then, as she was spotting sweetness all around her, she learned she was ill. A doctor she didn't know told her the grim diagnosis, and at first, she panicked.

But then this doctor she didn't know well told her about a playbook, and it included new breakthroughs patients just a few years ago had never even heard of.

Days passed, and she learned more. And the more she learned, the more hopeful she became. She told her precious beloveds that she would be receiving immunotherapy instead of chemotherapy and reminded them it was okay to be afraid, but it was even better to feel grateful. She said this:

> *You know, just ten years ago, the odds of surviving stage IV colon cancer for five years was just 15 percent. Can you imagine? It's not like that anymore. It's a remarkable time to be alive.*

Her teenagers will go to bed that night and google these immunotherapy drugs and instead of falling to sleep with voices of dread, they will be lifted up by angels, who will surround their dreaming hearts with hope.

Many days the fear overwhelmed her. In her uncertainty, she stumbled in the dark, rationalizing a way to betray even herself because there were times when the lanterns of her last room were dimmed by the lie that being in the last room ought to give her permission to embrace the idea of randomness rather than the miracle that all of this—all the beautiful and all the terrible—is an eternal story. It's a story shaped by faith to understand that the lights draw us closer to wonder. Only then can we renew our imagination so we can see its higher purpose: a forever aiming toward whatever is true, noble, and right; whatever is pure, lovely, and admirable; and anything excellent or praiseworthy.

* * *

I hold this mom and her terrific kids in my heart now, each day I receive these new drugs.

My last room is for her now.

My last room is full of purpose because Paul's enduring virtues have brought me ever closer to what awaits me after this room.

Frederick Buechner, whose words have been sprinkled through these pages, once meditated that the empty tomb was a stirring reminder that the worst thing isn't the last thing.

And this is why I now understand my last room is a triumphant bridge to the genuine beginning—a realm where Paul's virtues are in constant abundance. A kingdom of joy.

We see glimpses of heaven here in our many rooms, and I've seen these glimpses transform into breathtaking sightings.

I've seen a dolphin swim alongside a catamaran off the shores of Hawaii, escorting me to a cove full of tuxedo-clad fish with bright yellow fins.

I've seen Don care for me from a place of fragile brokenness and a heart of deep love.

I've seen Visser's suits.

I've seen Colocci come to every appointment focused entirely on me, focused entirely on finding me more time.

I've seen Ko listening with extraordinary empathy and wisdom.

I've seen my friends generously loving me in some of my loneliest days. How they flew in for chemo rounds and then came back for scans. How they let me tell very simple stories in a way that took two hours longer than necessary.

I've seen my mom devoted to the idea that my cancer will be cured. This is pure devotion. Moms know how to love their beloveds with unparalleled clarity, no matter what a scan says.

I've seen my dad teach me to love sports without clocks. To know that sitting next to his kids for nine innings can result in conversations that change lives.

I've seen how Jacquelline met my fear, faced it, and sketched out a plan to ease it.

I've seen how my sisters have tracked my every day, understanding that each matters. I've seen how my brother reached out to experts and experts who knew experts, one of whom helped connect me to the trial in which I'm now enrolled.

I've seen Sebastien's magnificent skills and discernment and his healing expertise extend my life. I've seen how his heart is even more gifted than his surgical hands and how my own shortcomings allowed an asymmetry to take hold when loneliness and fear of the last room became too heavy to endure.

I've seen Lucy dance, with her elegant arms outstretched, as if to say, *Come closer, this is how the angels surround us.*

I've seen Connor play his trumpet alongside other street musicians in Florence during a pandemic's peak, reminding us all that even the darkest days can contain tales of transcendent harmony and celebration to be passed down for generations.

I have seen all of these things. I have believed in all of these things. I have lived all of these things, fully, here in the last room.

And now I know all these moments, illuminated by an ancient letter, are miraculous preludes to what awaits me after this room. The scriptures tell us that Isaiah prophesized this:

> *Behold, I am doing a new thing; now it springs forth, do you not perceive it? I will make a way in the wilderness and rivers in the desert.*
>
> —ISAIAH 43:19 (NIV)

The prophecy speaks to the universally sacred reminder that all will be made new. There will forever be a new chapter in our stories, no matter our room. The Author of our stories trusts us—loves us—enough to walk alongside us as we discern our path forward, equipping us with lights to see even in the darkest shadows.

This room is bringing me ever closer to the greatest truth of all: the kingdom after this room has no disease, no tears, no fear. The longer I spend in the last room, the more I understand it's a magnificent bridge, because with every step through this brave in-between place, an enduring truth is revealed: Chaos has no place here. Only purpose, only an invitation to draw closer to these lights that will unveil a story whose narrative will creatively surpass our own imaginations.

The flickers of light that guide our time through all of the rooms of our lives illuminate our way, but they do something more.

They enchant. They create a stirring.

A desire to fall in love with this promise: You are healed. You are loved.

Your story is just now beginning.

Come and see.

ACKNOWLEDGMENTS

As it turns out, the last room is expansive; there is more room than you could imagine for visitors. When you knock on the door of a dear friend's last room, know that he or she might be a mess inside. It may take a little while to tidy up the room for a visit, so do this—wait patiently just outside the door. It may open, and when it does, there will be a place for you to sit alongside your last-room friend. You may say the wrong thing. You may want to bring some kind of gift, and you may guess wrong (there are so many new socks in the last room!).

Come anyway. Try anyway. You're bringing your big and often messy heart to this place—your love—which is exactly what the last room needs. (A note to fellow last-room dwellers: Give your sweet friends who say the wrong thing a little pass to be clumsy as they get settled. We're all doing our best.)

My last room has been filled with some of the most remarkable souls anyone could hope to know, and many provided beautiful insights as these pages began to form.

Andrea Elliott gave me an early vote of confidence and reminded me that writers rarely tell people who have cancer to write a book ("we bring a meal instead," she said).

Other writers and storytellers who read my blog in the earliest days also found ways to encourage me. Dick Tofel, David Bornstein, Dave Isay, Amanda Ripley, and Sarabeth Berman whispered in my ear to explore this idea in earnest. Nicola Wheir provided expert input to way too early drafts.

For more than a decade, my colleagues at Emerson Collective have told the best stories, because they've helped put the best stories in motion. Listening to them helped me find my own voice for these pages. Peter Lattman, Evan Smith, Patrick D'Arcy, Marcy Stech, Hannah Stonebraker, Megan Dino, and Anne Marie Burgoyne have upped my game every day. Alex Simon read early drafts and indulged long conversations about it all. She discovered stories underneath the stories I thought I would initially tell. She's excellent at that kind of thing.

Arne Duncan has chosen to dedicate his life to walking alongside young men in Chicago who live far too close to the last room. He's taught me how to listen, how to learn, how to persevere.

Laurene Powell has an uncanny ability to strategically frame the hardest problems by drawing intimately close to the story of an individual in need. Her fearlessness, imagination, and unending empathy inspire me every day.

If there is a perk to dwelling in the last room, it's that friends from chapters long ago arrive, just in time. Ashley Pearson Erol and Tiffany Bendetti began as college roommates; they are now soulmates. Kimberly Donahue, Staci Darmody, and Rosemarie Springer found me after twenty-five years and made me a better person as a result. Valisa Smith never let me go.

Other friends who have moved through all my many life rooms found a way to draw even closer in this last one. Libby Cannizzaro, Susie Chang, Ellen Pitera, Michelle Knott, Amy Meyer Lovejoy, and Ann Holladay didn't just visit my last room; they stayed a good long while. They made it far less terrifying. Tracy Schutte helped furnish the place with remarkable love and grace.

Patti Buck and Julia Molise are dear friends who have raised exceptional daughters. They also know how to show up to an ER, making a horrifying day far less so. Jim Fabio and John Burman brought laughter to the last room, effortlessly.

Jacquelline Fuller didn't just attend medical appointments, she also took detailed notes. And then let me talk for hours about what we just heard, nodding along in solidarity.

Brigitte Lacombe welcomed me into her studio and her heart. Both are magical places.

My medical team is marvelous. I'm here because of their tenacity and brilliance. Natalia Colocci, Brendan Visser, Andrew Ko, Bridget Keenan, Julia Marx, Sunil Sharma, Carol Guarnieri, and Mary Feng—along with dozens of nurses and schedulers—are among the world's finest healers.

Experts from the Colorectal Cancer Alliance entered my story at the exact right time, as they do for thousands of patients each year. My thanks to Michael Sapienza for founding this organization and dedicating his life to easing, and someday ending, the burden of this awful disease (Michael would remind me to tell you that everyone forty-five and older ought to get a colonoscopy).

Pierre Theodore offered friendship and expert advice from the first hour of my diagnosis.

Don Low cared for me with a big and beautiful heart when I got sick; Connor and Lucy will always soar in part because of his joyous spirit.

Dwayne Betts invited me to commiserate with him while I was writing. Commiserating with a poet is never not delightful.

I'm grateful to my new friends at Hachette, especially Lauren Marino and Niyati Patel, who found ways to strengthen my prose and sharpen my thinking.

My agent, Mark Tauber, is a skilled adviser and an even better friend. You couldn't ask for a smarter advocate.

Dale Hanson Bourke has been a mentor and friend for more than twenty-five years. She emerged as an early reader, dogged thought partner, and brilliant gut checker throughout this project.

Shirley Mullen brought many gifts to my last room, most notably wisdom, clarity, grace, and devotion. She embodies the miracle of accompaniment.

I give thanks for my family. For my mom, who navigated the sudden death of my terrific dad just two weeks after my diagnosis and her stalwart confidence in best outcomes. My siblings and their spouses—Steve Beard, Julie Beard, Mindy Smith,

Kyle Smith—live out Paul's virtues in ways that make all of our lives brighter, and better. Julie, especially, has shown me how to embrace my story, no matter how complicated the plot.

And, finally, to Connor and Lucy. Someday you will tell your stories in the most magical ways. I will be listening.